Keys2Concussions

A Complete Program Guide for Concussions

Serving You:

From Impact to Recovery

Concussion Facts

The mysteries of concussions are as great as the debts of the brain itself; however, much scientific research and studies have been done to shed some light on these previously uncharted waters.

Even with its recent popularity, a 2015 Harris poll reports that nearly 90% of Americans cannot correctly define a concussion and are not familiar with the post-concussion syndrome that can follow.

Records show that up to 3.8 million sports related concussions happen within a year, and according to the CDC, an estimated number of over 170,000 children under the age of 19 are treated annually in emergency departments for traumatic brain injuries including concussions.

According to the DVBIC, the Defense Department's office responsible for tracking traumatic brain injury (TBI) data in the U.S. military, since 2000, 361,092 military enlisted have sustained a traumatic brain injury.

With such astronomically high statistics, we can no longer afford to be un-educated and un-prepared in the face of concussions.

TBI's including concussions are the number one cause of unintentional death and disability among children. They rob professional athletes of their livelihood, and their footprints torment our heroes and veterans of war.

Mission: Providing nutritional options, answers, and support to individuals and their families impacted by concussions and TBI's.

IMPROVE YOUR BRAIN HEALTH NOW WITHOUT READING A WORD

https://keys2eating.myshopify.com/products/brain-health-support-kit

Welcome to the Concussion Recovery Guide!

You are not alone! Hundreds of thousands of people have faced concussions and TBI's. There is a community, a family and a network of support here for you!

Your about to start your journey with continued learning and by creating a very specific step-by-step concussion protocol plan to fit your needs.

It's important that you do everything you can to take advantage of all the training you're going to get during these challenging times.

It's also very important that you not only learn but are able to implement the information and steps you will be provided.

This concussion recovery system is your guide through the entire concussion recovery process, from impact to recovery.

FINAL NOTE:

It's important to not get over whelmed, stressed out or to give up. Remain patient and persistent while you learn what works best, this will help ensure your success through this program. Remember, no two concussions are ever the same, even in the same individual, and everyone's personal experience will be different. This plan is designed to help you create a system that works best for you and your situation. Always remember, you are not alone! We look forward to hearing from you.

In this book you will learn:

Section One
Describing, Identifying, and Testing for Concussions and Post-Concussion Syndrome.

Section Two

"How to feed the brain"

How to eat to help the brain heal after a concussion, including a complete meal plan with recipes

Section 3

"The Aftermath"

A reintegration plan; emotional healing, how to work with educators and employers, and the creation of your personalized concussion protocol plan.

My Son's Story: WATCH HIS VIDEO HERE

https://www.youtube.com/watch?v=CcZNU5WEtwM

"I feel so dumb; I don't know what's wrong with me." These were the words my son told me after suffering from his first concussion unbeknownst to me.

One stereotypical afternoon my son came bouncing down the stairs as any normal active boy might do then all of the sudden I heard an awful sound of banging and thumping then an outburst of screams from my son.

His younger sister came running saying, "mommy brother fell down the stairs and is on the floor."

I went hurriedly around the corner and helped him up off the wood floor. Staggering, I helped him to the couch to assess the injury.

I had no first-hand experience with concussions so I performed all of the typical and very cliché concussion tests. (Looking back my ignorance at the time is very humbling to say the least) I looked at his pupils with a light and asked him to follow my finger with his eyes. He didn't pass out or vomit, so I thought we were in the clear.

That my friends was it, the extent of my concussion screening and apparent my education on the subject. I had him lay back on the couch and ice his head. He laid there for all of about 10 minutes before his friends came ringing the doorbell requesting him to come out and play soccer. I asked him how he was feeling and with no visible marks, this active 9-year-old boy begged to go outside to play soccer with his friends. Naturally, I thought he must be ok, and released him to his free will.

After a persistent headache, the following day I took him in for a CAT scan and evaluation. The CAT scan results came back normal, and it was not ruled a concussion, at this time.

It wasn't until three days later when the memory loss was apparent, and we realized the severity of the concussion.

Things quickly got worse, headaches, memory loss, lethargy, depression, anxiety, sleeplessness, and even seizures.

It was the height of the hockey playoffs which he had followed religiously with his father. He knew every player by name. However, all of that knowledge had suddenly disappeared.   We realized something was wrong when he could not follow a conversation and repeatedly would begin speaking only to say never mind. He literally, was at a loss for words. He repeatedly asked for the time and had a perplexed look fixed on his face when we would engage him in conversation.

Anxiety began to set in as he drew more and more blanks and realized he couldn't remember people or events that we could. "I feel dumb," he said, as he could no longer complete his math homework. He forgot all of the multiplication facts he had just recently mastered.

Since in my son's case we were unaware that he suffered a concussion, so we did not follow the proper concussion protocol and steps to protect him from more neurological strain, and post-concussive syndrome soon became his reality.

Severe migraines and vertigo lasted for the first month, while sleep disturbances became more evident and emotionally he was not himself. He was placed on a homebound school program since he could perform only minimal tasks while symptoms persisted. However, to my surprise, the school did not have a concussion plan ready to implement. I was left to educate his educators on his condition even though, I was still learning.

The school believed that since outwardly he appeared to be fine, and projected the attitude of disbelief of his expressed continued symptoms.

Due to the nature of concussion and post-concussion syndrome, the majority of the battle was an inner struggle with no outside visible marks. Because of this, he was often accused of "milking it" or "making things up." I believe this was partly due to the lack of information, education and complexity of this subject.

Unfortunately, many people, including myself, did not understand this after-math of a concussion and it was a long, difficult journey. After initially being cleared from his concussion, the dizziness, ringing in the ears (tinnitus), and headaches became so severe they would be completely debilitating at times. It was all he could do to sit up and the light sensitivity was so extreme that he just wanted to lay in a dark room.

It was heart breaking for me to see him like this and I was forced to watch as he became more and more dejected just wanting to return to his normal self.

After time went by with these continued symptoms his neurologist and concussion specialist suggested he be seen. We made the two hour commute and he was admitted into the hospital for concussion evaluation and treatment.

I remember we both felt so relieved expecting to find this amazing cure that would return him to the physically active boy he used to be.

In efforts to reduce his headaches the doctors administered an anti-epileptic drug called Depakote (valproic acid) via IV. Depakote is a common drug used to treat migraines, seizures, and mood disorders in children and adults.

Initially, I wasn't concerned and trusted the doctors, after all up to this point it had been al misery. I just wanted him to have some relief.

After the first hour of receiving the drug he began to say that he was having a difficult time moving his legs. I thought maybe he just needed to stretch and move about a bit. He hung his legs over the side of the bed struggling and stood up very slowly. He looked as though he was balancing on wobbly stilts.

I asked him if he was ok and he said his legs felt like they were too small for his body.

I thought that was odd and we contacted the nurse to discuss this with the doctor.

They didn't seem concerned and continued administering the Depakote via IV. At about 2 ½ hours into the treatment he got up to try and use the bathroom but his legs buckled underneath him and he reach out to the IV pole to catch himself. I offered my assistance but he assertively told me he could do it himself. His frustration yet persistence was very evident so I stepped back. He was not used to having to depend on so much help and did not like it at all. He proceeded to the bathroom holding onto the pole dragging his legs across the floor. I alerted the nurse again regarding the increase in the lack of mobility to his legs but they continued the Depakote drip without concern.

After 6 hours of treatment, he lost complete mobility in his legs and couldn't even stand by himself. His description of the feeling was consistent and he said that he felt like he had little legs and they couldn't hold up his body.

I was done at this point and had the nurses call his neurologist to discontinue the treatment. The neurologists insisted to me this was not the result of the drugs, as they had not come across such a reaction before.

As any mama bear might do, I completed research through the night on this drug and came across a girl my son's age who had a similar "drunken like response" as it was explained, when given the same dose of Depakote through an IV.

The next morning he still had no mobility in his legs, and his emotional state was declining rapidly, and after enough persistence, they granted me my wish and took him off of the Depakote. It was unfortunate that it was not done without a degree of condescending treatment.

Almost to the minute of the initial dosage, within 6 hours of stopping the medication, he could walk again.

During this time not only did he lose the use of his legs but he also experienced negative psychological effects from the drug and became very depressed and anxious.

After this situation I saw the frustration and sadness in my son's eyes. He wasn't getting better, his teachers didn't believe him the medicine the doctors gave him didn't work and even they questioned the validity of his loss of mobility. I seemed to be the only one who knew him and was with him around the clock to notice the truth.

When he asked me what we were going to do I could not let him down and there was no way I was going to tell him we were out of options. I knew that I must find another option. It was at this place in our concussion journey that The Complete Concussion Protocol was be created.

My son's relationships with concussions would not end with one, partly due to the severity of the initial concussion. Research shows that once you receive a concussion your chances of getting another one increase up to 3X and it takes much less of a severe hit to the head each time.

He suffered another concussion in 2015 at school when a classmate playfully pulled his chair out from underneath him sending him falling back hitting his head on a desk.

The third concussion occurred in 2016 by what was considered a mild blow to the head during football practice. Both times the familiar feeling of concussion filled his head, and he was immediately evaluated, and the proper steps in our concussion protocol began.

Never again would I make the same mistake, and be caught off guard by a concussion. I was in control of the situation and ready to help by son. I will never forget that feeling of helplessness. No price can be placed on being prepared once a concussion takes place.

It was through these experiences that I met other individuals also suffering from the effects of concussions and I realized there was a lack of adequate information and direction for those needing answers, like myself after my son's first concussion.

I also realized how many people were so unaware of the debilitating effects that concussions and TBI's could bring.

The most shocking discovery for me was when I learned of a concussion's silent partner, this mysterious secondary injury that secretly takes place after the initial injury.

It was this reason that I sought to create the Concussion Protocol. As I began to implement the information I had learned and researched in my own son's life, I experienced bitter sweet emotions. I was elated and grateful to have answers and a plan for my son, while at the same time, I was angry that I could not find this information in its totality after his initial concussion.

It was during that epiphany that I realized, the information I used to help my son needed to be documented and put to print for others out there struggling and searching for solutions and answers.

I felt compelled to share what I had found and no one else was talking about, at least in and around my circle.

The information in this book is a composition of scientific and medical research, case studies, and real life applications brought together over a span of 5 years.

I am so excited for you, that you have found this information, because I know it works! I have such gratitude in knowing my son didn't suffer in vain, and our struggles brought answers that can help others.

Please join our Facebook community if you haven't already. People need people! Welcome to our community!   https://www.facebook.com/Keys2Concussions/

Important note from the author:

This book is not meant to treat, diagnose, or to take the place of medical attention for a traumatic brain injury or possible concussion. This book is for information purposes only.

If you are reading this and either you or a loved one has suffered what you believe to be a concussion and have not yet been evaluated by a medical professional, STOP reading and seek medical attention immediately! Head trauma should not be self-diagnosed and could be life threatening. In no way should this book be considered a substitute for a medical diagnoses or medical treatment. Once you or your loved one is evaluated by a doctor, re-connect with us for education, real solutions, and the quickest path to recovery.

Preface

We often take our brain for granted until we are reminded just how depended on it we are. The brain is a complex computing device that even the fastest computers in the world cannot emulate at the same speed. In 2014 a group of computer researchers from Japan and Germany was able to simulate one second of brain activity. However, it took 40 minutes and the use of 82,944 processors.

In the upcoming chapters you will take a journey inside the brain to get a glimpse of this extraordinary computing device. You will learn about the brains unmatched intellectual power and its' intricate detailed workings exposing the vulnerabilities.

We are fearfully and wonderfully made and medical science still has much to uncover; however, some truths have been proven.

Journey with me now into the brain and discover what goes on in the brain during and after a concussion

Section One
Describing, Identifying, and Testing for Concussions and Post-Concussion Syndrome.

Chapter 1

What is a concussion and the different types of concussions?

Concussions have found themselves in the spot-light quite a bit lately. Surfacing research, movies and unfortunate bouts of suicides from prominent athletes are merely a few reasons for their popularity.

Even with this recent exposure, a 2015 Harris Poll reports that nearly 90% of Americans cannot correctly define a concussion and are not familiar with the post-concussive syndrome that can follow.

90% of population cannot properly define a concussion

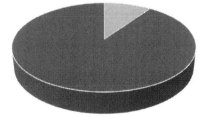

- ■ **Properly define a concussion**
- ■ **Cannot properly define a concussion**

Each year there are a reported 1.7 million civilian brain injuries in the United States. In the military from 2000 through 2012, more than 266,000 service members sustained a TBI. Brain injury has become known as the signature wound of the wars in Iraq and Afghanistan.

My goal for you is that by the end of this book you will not be part of that 90%. You will know what a concussion is, what happens to the brain during and after a concussion, and how to help the brain recover if a concussion takes place.

First, let's answer the question, what is a concussion?

A concussion is a type of mild TBI (traumatic brain injury) usually identified as some form of a blow to the head, the head hitting off of another item, a penetrating wound to the head, or severe movement and jerking of the head.

> ➢ Blow to head
> ➢ Head hitting another item
> ➢ Penetrating wound to head
> ➢ Severe movement and jerking of head

Head injuries are classified as either impact or non- impact injuries. If the head makes direct contact or impact with an object like in a car accident, fight, or fall, it is classified as impact. If the injury occurs as a non-impact force such as blast waves as in a military grade IED, or rapid acceleration and deceleration which can also happen in a car accident, or like in SBS, Shaking Baby Syndrome it is classified as non-impact.

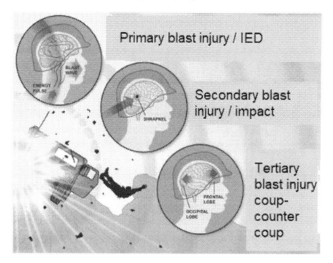

There are different degrees of a concussion and TBI's (traumatic brain injuries). The damage to the brain is contingent upon the severity of the brain injury and the location of impact. Currently, the severity of TBI's and concussions are categorized based on the Glasgow Coma Scale (GCS). On the GCS patients are scored by clinical symptoms. The scale rating is mild (score: 13-15), moderate (score: 9-12) or severe (score: <9).

Glasgow Coma Scale		
Response	Scale	Score
Eye Opening Response	Eyes open spontaneously	4 Points
	Eyes open to verbal command, speech, or shout	3 Points
	Eyes open to pain (not applied to face)	2 Points
	No eye opening	1 Point
Verbal Response	Oriented	5 Points
	Confused conversation, but able to answer questions	4 Points
	Inappropriate responses, words discernible	3 Points
	Incomprehensible sounds or speech	2 Points
	No verbal response	1 Point
Motor Response	Obeys commands for movement	6 Points
	Purposeful movement to painful stimulus	5 Points
	Withdraws from pain	4 Points
	Abnormal (spastic) flexion, decorticate posture	3 Points
	Extensor (rigid) response, decerebrate posture	2 Points
	No motor response	1 Point
Minor Brain Injury = 13-15 points; **Moderate Brain Injury** = 9-12 points; **Severe Brain Injury** = 3-8 points		

Most individuals do not know that within TBI's and concussions there are two stages of injury. The primary and secondary injury. The primary is the initial injury that causes the brain to be displaced within the skull, while the secondary injury is the continued effects that happen in the brain as a result of the primary injury. The secondary injuries gradually occur as a consequence of ongoing cellular events that cause further damage.

Both, have unique disturbances and symptoms associated with them. Because most individuals are completely unaware a secondary injury exists, the symptoms associated with it occur without explanation of their existence. The focus is usually placed on the initial injury or hit to the head. Unfortunately, sometimes the initial or primary injury does not show any symptoms and goes undiagnosed, therefore, leaving behind, no explanation when symptoms occur.

You must be informed regarding what takes place in the brain during the secondary injury to properly treat a concussion.

We will cover the secondary injury later in this chapter, but, before we get ahead of ourselves, let's first cover the brain as it lives in the skull.

The Brain inside the Skull

Our skulls are only a quarter inch thick. Male skulls are a little thicker, which is fortunate because statistics show that men tend to get TBI's more often than women. However, research also shows that it can take females longer to recovery from a concussion than males.

The skull is both protective and restricting. It is the brain's best defense, but also, its greatest risk in times of trauma.

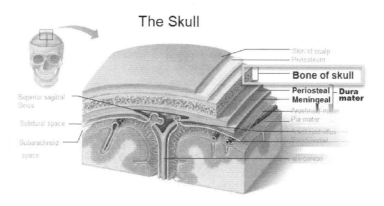

The Skull

Surrounding the brain is a rubbery light clear layer of tissue called the dura mater. This layer helps protect the brain from moving around too much. Beneath the dura mater is another layer called the arachnoid layer, which looks and feels like moist cotton candy. The dura mater, the arachnoid layer, and another layer, the pia mater, all form what is known as the meninges. The meninges keeps the brain floating inside the skull. If these layers get infected, ripped, or torn, it can cause severe damage to the brain.

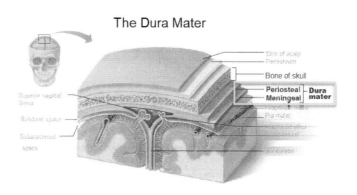

The Dura Mater

Though it was known fact, that trauma to the brain could induce hemorrhaging, swelling, coma and even death; new supporting research has concluded that even what was previously considered minor blows to the head can do much more damage than initially presumed.

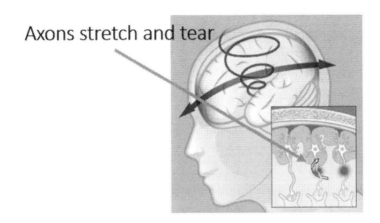

Axons stretch and tear

Medical scientists have learned that much of this has to do with the secondary injury that takes place after the primary or initial injury.

It does not take a strong force to cause damage to the brain and often there can be no immediate signs or symptoms that any injury has taken place.

It is for this reason that concussion education and awareness is necessary for the population to be vigilant in protecting one of its most valuable possessions.

If we do not take care of our brains, our brains will not be able to take care of us as we age.

Furthermore, research has also revealed that age does matter; especially in certain sports like football as young boys do not have the muscle development yet to adequately support the head during impact. Also, a developing and growing brain can have significant setbacks in the developmental stages if a severe enough concussion or TBI takes place, and it takes a more minimal hit to cause injury.

Even common whiplash like movements on your favorite rollercoaster or in horseplay can send the brain smacking the inside of the skull walls initiating tearing and shearing of brain axons damaging the brain and inducing a powerful secondary injury.

Types of head injuries

Every brain injury is unique and scary to each individual. There are two basic types of head injuries, open head injuries, and closed head injuries.

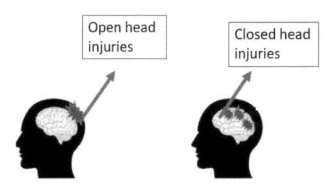

Both closed and open head injuries can be classified as either concussions or traumatic brain injuries contingent upon the severity of the injury. TBI's or traumatic brain injuries are classified as more severe than a concussion and are categorized by serious symptoms such as prolonged unconsciousness or coma.

As previously discussed above, all of which are categorized on the Glasgow Coma Scale.

Concussions are considered a mild TBI. However, they can still result in a period of unconsciousness, and be debilitating, and even life-threatening at times if swelling or fluid on the brain is present.

In an open head injury, the scalp bleeds a lot creating a chaotic mess. The brain is such a detailed yet complicated tangle of matter that it can be extremely difficult to remove pieces of scalp lodged into its' tissue. Brain surgery can be placed right up there with rocket science.

Closed head injuries are a little different but can be just as complicated and vicious in nature. During a closed head injury often the brain slams against one portion of the skull then bounces against the opposite side of the wall.

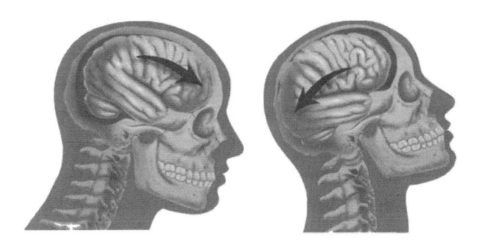

This action is called a "coup-contra coup" injury, where two injuries occur from one single blow. The most common form of a closed head injury is a concussion. After the primary injury or impact, the secondary injuries can continue for up to 48 hours. During this time there are chemical disturbances in the brain that lead to an increase in symptoms like fatigue, sleep problems, loss of concentration, mood swings, headaches and general feelings of being ill.

Any time the brain suffers a violent force or movement, the soft, floating brain is slammed against the skull's uneven and rough interior. The internal lower surface of the skull is a rough, bony structure that often damages the fragile tissues within the brain as it moves across the bone surface. The brain may even rotate during this process. This friction can also stretch and strain the brain's threadlike nerve cells called axons.

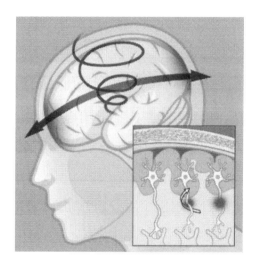

When the head has a rotational movement during trauma, the brain moves, twists, and experiences forces that cause differential movement of brain matter. This sudden movement or direct force applied to the head can set the brain tissue in motion even though the brain is well protected by the skull and very resilient.

Upon impact and severe motion brain cells called neurons can be stretched and often squeezed completely tearing. Neural cells require a precise balance and distance between cells to efficiently signal and send messages between cells. The stretching and squeezing of brain cells from these forces can change the precise balance, which can result in problems in how the brain processes information.

Different cognitive functions can be altered depending on the area of the brain that has been effected by the trauma.

Though the stretching and swelling of the axons may seem relatively minor or microscopic, the impact on the brain's neurological circuits can be significant. Even a "mild" injury can result in significant physiological damage, behavioral and emotional imbalances, and cognitive deficits.

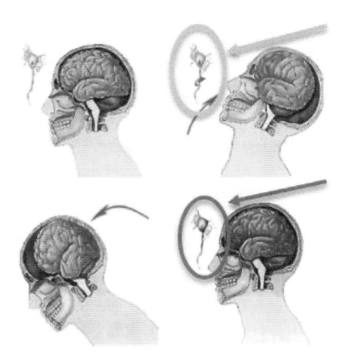

If a person's head is whipped around, a small tearing effect called shearing occurs throughout the brain, resulting in a diffuse axonal injury. Axons are the hair-like extensions of nerve cells that transmit messages. In a diffuse axonal injury, the messages either get mixed up, or they don't come through at all.

After seeing what takes place in the brain along with the damages caused to the brain cells, I would like to touch on a current issue in society today and take the time to bring awareness regarding Shaking Baby Syndrome (SBS).

It is for the reason above, why shaking a baby, or young child can be so dangerous. Even innocently tossing them up in the air too rough, or bouncing them around to rigorously can do damage.

SBS, Shaking Baby Syndrome

SBS or shaking baby syndrome is a form of child abuse that occurs when an adult or older child violently shakes a baby or young child. It only takes a few seconds of shaking to cause permanent damage.

SBS is usually caused by a frustrated parent or caregiver who shakes a baby or young child when it won't stop crying or because of some other stressful situation. During this moment there is usually no intent to cause harm to the child. However, no intent does not result in no harm.

Shaking can cause brain injury, cerebral palsy, blindness, hearing loss, learning and behavior problems, seizures, paralysis, and death. It is estimated that 1000 - 3000 children in the United States suffer from SBS each year, and one out of four victims to not survive and an astounding 80% of survivors suffer from permanent damage.

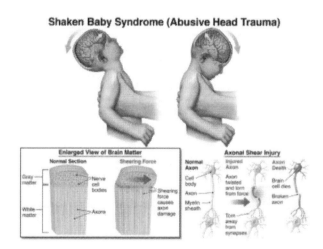

Sports and Concussions

Sports are often a topic of concern when it comes to the fear of concussions and the will to prevent them.

High school football accounts for 47 percent of all reported sports concussions, with 33 percent of concussions occurring during practice.

My son's third concussion was the only sports-related concussion, and it occurred during football practice by another teammate while they were running drills.

Football is not the only sport where athletes suffer from concussions. Though football is the most common sport with concussion risk for males at 75%, soccer isn't too far behind in numbers with a 50% risk for concussion in both males and females. 78% of concussions occur during games (as opposed to practices).

Concussion tops the list of injuries sustained by high school cheerleaders as the once-tame sideline activity becomes more daring and competitive, a new U.S. study finds.

Some studies suggest that females are twice as likely to sustain a concussion as males.

The most commonly reported symptoms immediately following concussions for injured athletes are 85% complain of a headache and 70-80% have dizziness.

A shocker is that an estimated 47% of athletes do not report feeling any symptoms after a concussive blow.

It is important for athletes to be able to recognize the symptoms of concussions and have the power to choose their brain health over game points and having to appear tough.

The following are some examples to help put impacts into perspective:

- A professional football player will receive an estimated 900 to 1500 blows to the head during a season

- Impact speed of professional boxers punch: 20mph

- Impact speed of a football player tackling a stationary player: 25mph

- Impact speed of a soccer ball being headed by a player: 70mph

Tips to help children and teens avoid concussions and head trauma

Babies

• Always make sure that your baby or child rides in an approved child safety seat or booster seat each time he travels in a vehicle.

• Never place your baby on a chair, table or another high place while they are in a car seat or baby carrier.

Use Approved Car Seats

Never place baby seats or carriers on high places

• Use the safety straps on changing tables, grocery carts, and high chairs.

• Do not allow children to carry your baby.

• Do not use baby walkers that have wheels. These can tip over and cause harm. Use a baby activity center without wheels instead.

Toddlers

• Childproof your home to protect him from falls.

• Secure large pieces of furniture, TVs, and appliances to the floor to prevent them from tipping over on your child. Use anti-tip brackets if needed.

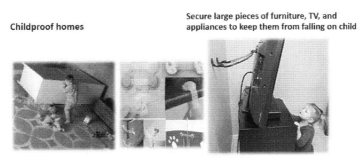

Childproof homes

Secure large pieces of furniture, TV, and appliances to keep them from falling on child

• Lock windows and screens. On upper floors, install safety bars that can keep your child from falling out of windows, but can be removed in case of fire.

• Use safety gates at the top and bottom of stairs until your child can go up and down safely on his own. Keep stairs free of clutter.

Secure windows allowing for fire escape

Use safety gates

• Make sure your toddler wears an approved bike helmet and sits in an approved seat when riding a bike with you

• Watch your child closely on the playground. Make sure play equipment is in good working order. The playground surface should be made of at least 12 inches deep shredded rubber, mulch or fine sand. Avoid harder surfaces like asphalt, concrete, grass and soil.

Child safety helmets when riding on bikes

Playground safety

Older children and teens

• Make sure your child wears a seatbelt every time he rides in a vehicle. Children under 13 years of age are safer in the back seat.

• Make sure he wears the correct helmet when he rides a bike, skateboards or takes part in other active sports.

Make sure children and teens wear seat belts

Helmets while on bikes, skateboards or active sports

The Complete Concussion Protocol is your guide from "Impact to Recovery". The first 48 hours following a concussion are crucial in determining the impact and long term effects on the concussed individual. No concussion or TBI is the same. They are as unique as their victims. The Complete Concussion Protocol is supported by cutting edge medical research, detailing what you don't know about concussions, and the metabolic upset, including the neurological cascade that follows during the first 48 hours. Through simple explanations, supported by scientific medical research, The Complete Concussion Protocol will walk you through the concussion journey from the initial impact through the recovery stages.

In section one of the book, you will learn what to do and what not to do in the first 48 hours following a concussion. You will learn how to identify concussions and post-concussion syndrome; as well as, what tests doctors use to diagnose a Concussion and Post-Concussion Syndrome. In the book, you will receive a step by step symptom tracker and plan for safe recovery.

In section two of the book, you will learn how to eat to help the brain heal after a concussion, including food lists, itemizing what to eat and what not to eat to best aid in brain health. With The Complete Concussion Protocol, you will also gain access to the resources on the Keys2Concussions and Keys2Eating websites including recipes to help guide you in your complete recovery.

In section three of the book, you will receive a personalized reintegration plan. This section includes emotional healing; how to work with educators and employers; and guides you through the creation of your own personalized concussion protocol plan.

This book utilizes helpful links, and PDF documents with instructions to walk you through the planning and recovery stages. With our veterans in mind, the brain health recommendations and reintegration program techniques were developed to support our heroes and to help encourage their efforts in recovery from PTSD.

FINAL NOTE:
Doctors have a saying when it comes to concussions and TBIs; "If you've seen one concussion, you've seen one concussion". Concussions are as unique as the individual that suffers from it, as no two concussions are ever the same, even in the same individual, everyone's personal experience will be different. This plan is designed to help you create your system that works best for you and your situation. Remain patient and persistent while you implement and learn what works best; this will help ensure your success through this concussion recovery system.

Download your copy of The Complete Concussion Protocol, and start your journey towards recovery and better health today. The Complete Concussion Protocol is your guide from "Impact to Recovery". The first 48 hours following a concussion are crucial in determining the impact and long term effects on the concussed individual. No concussion or TBI is the same. They are as unique as their victims. The Complete Concussion Protocol is supported by cutting edge medical research, detailing what you don't know about concussions, and the metabolic upset, including the neurological cascade that follows during the first 48 hours. Through simple explanations, supported by scientific medical research, The Complete Concussion Protocol will walk you through the concussion journey from the initial impact through the recovery stages.

In section one of the book, you will learn what to do and what not to do in the first 48 hours following a concussion. You will learn how to identify concussions and post-concussion syndrome; as well as, what tests doctors use to diagnose a Concussion and Post-Concussion Syndrome. In the book, you will receive a step by step symptom tracker and plan for safe recovery.

In section two of the book, you will learn how to eat to help the brain heal after a concussion, including food lists, itemizing what to eat and what not to eat to best aid in brain health. With The Complete Concussion Protocol, you will also gain access to the resources on the Keys2Concussions and Keys2Eating websites including recipes to help guide you in your complete recovery.

In section three of the book, you will receive a personalized reintegration plan. This section includes emotional healing; how to work with educators and employers; and guides you through the creation of your own personalized concussion protocol plan.

This book utilizes helpful links, and PDF documents with instructions to walk you through the planning and recovery stages. With our veterans in mind, the brain health recommendations and reintegration program techniques were developed to support our heroes and to help encourage their efforts in recovery from

PTSD.

FINAL NOTE:
Doctors have a saying when it comes to concussions and TBIs; "If you've seen one concussion, you've seen one concussion". Concussions are as unique as the individual that suffers from it, as no two concussions are ever the same, even in the same individual, everyone's personal experience will be different. This plan is designed to help you create your system that works best for you and your situation. Remain patient and persistent while you implement and learn what works best; this will help ensure your success through this concussion recovery system.

Download your copy of The Complete Concussion Protocol, and start your journey towards recovery and better health today.

• All-terrain vehicles (ATVs) should only be used by teens, age 16 years and over. They need to wear a motorcycle style helmet and should never have passengers on the ATV with them.

ATV's and all-terrain vehicles should be used by those 16yrs and older using motorcycle style helmets.

Functions of the different parts of the brain

The brain is highly functioning organ that controls your entire body, divided into two parts. The left brain is responsible for controlling the right side of your body. It is also responsible for things such as reading, writing, arithmetic, and memory retrieval, which is bringing back things that have already happened in the past. One thing that is special about the left brain is that it is very detailed. The left brain helps to recall the specific parts of thought, though only in a language format. It also remembers little things such as the rules of the English language, or whatever language you may speak.

In contrast, the right brain is responsible for controlling the left side of the body. The right brain is also seen as the creative side. It controls and contributes to activities like art, music, and nonverbal actions. Memory of sounds and sights is stored and recalled on the right side of the brain.

Below is a diagram of the functions of the different part of the brain to show you what areas of the brain perform specific tasks.

> The brain is divided into two parts
> Left brain controls the right side of your body
> Left brain is responsible for reading, writing, arithmetic, memory retrieval, language
> Right brain controls the left side of your body
> Right brain is seen as the creative side, contributes to activities like art, music, personality

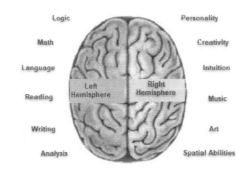

Chapter 2

How to Identify a Concussion

Concussion Signs, Symptoms, and Myths Surrounding a Concussion

Concussion signs and symptoms

The signs and symptoms of a concussion can be trivial to diagnose and may not be immediately apparent.

For example, with my son's first concussion he initially seemed to be fine and requested to go outside and play. Furthermore, it's reported that 47% of athletes don't report feeling any symptoms immediately following a concussive blow, but once symptoms appear they can last for days, weeks or even longer with post-concussive syndrome. According to the Mayo Clinic, Common symptoms after a

47% of Concussed Athletes Don't Report Any Signs and Symptoms After Initial Blow.

■ No Symptoms

concussive traumatic brain injury are headache, loss of memory (amnesia) or confusion. If there is amnesia, it may or may not follow a loss of consciousness, usually involves the loss of memory of the event that caused the concussion, but the memory loss may not be immediately apparent, as in the case of my son.

Signs and symptoms of a concussion may include:

- Headache or a feeling of pressure in the head
- Temporary loss of consciousness
- Confusion or feeling as if in a fog
- Amnesia surrounding the traumatic event
- Dizziness or "seeing stars"
- Ringing in the ears
- Nausea

- Vomiting
- Slurred speech
- Delayed response to questions
- Appearing dazed
- Fatigue

Some symptoms of concussions may be immediate or delayed in onset by hours or days after injury, such as:

- Concentration and memory complaints
- Irritability and other personality changes
- Sensitivity to light and noise
- Sleep disturbances
- Psychological adjustment problems and depression
- Disorders of taste and smell

Symptoms in children

Head trauma is very common in young children. But concussions can be difficult to recognize in infants and toddlers because they may not be able to describe how they feel. Nonverbal clues of a concussion may include:

- Appearing dazed
- Listlessness and tiring easily
- Irritability and crankiness
- Loss of balance and unsteady walking
- Crying excessively
- Change in eating or sleeping patterns
- Lack of interest in favorite toys

Concussion Myths

✓ *Someone has to pass out or vomit to have suffered a concussion.*

A major myth and misconception are that someone must have either passed out or vomited to have suffered a concussion. That couldn't be further from the truth. In fewer than 10% of sports-related concussion, the individual passes out. Concussions can be difficult to diagnose, especially when dealing with younger children who can either not yet communicate or are developing the ability to effectively communicate their symptoms. A diagnostic test by a physician should always be done. A danger with head trauma in adults is that while they may temporarily feel ok, swelling and hemorrhaging can occur later. Many of you might remember the TV personality who hit his head on an overhead luggage compartment and died later that day due to bleeding on the brain.

✓ *Someone has to throw up to have received a concussion*

In my son's case, he neither blacked out nor threw up, and the memory loss was not made apparent for three days. His initial complaints were a constant headache, and a he was feeling dumb when he was trying to complete school work.

✓ *You have to keep someone awake if they have hit their head*

The following is clarification regarding keeping someone awake after a head injury. Recent research has stated that there is no benefit to keeping someone awake after a concussion, and it is no longer recommended. In fact, people with a concussion need to sleep to recover.

The reason for this was before CAT scans were widely available, the only way to know if someone had life-threatening brain bleeding was to observe him or her for a decrease in the level of alertness that resulted from the blood pressing on vital brain structures. This usually happened within six hours of the injury so it was thought that if you could keep someone awake, you could prevent them from lapsing into a coma. Now it is known to be impossible, due to the fact, that a coma is not preventable by merely keeping someone awake.

However, it should be noted, anyone getting very sleepy following and within six hours of a brain injury should be brought to the emergency room for a head CT scan immediately.

Rather than keep someone awake, it is suggested to wake up a concussed person every 3 to 4 hours during the night just to evaluate changes in symptoms and rule out any possibility of hematoma or bleeding in the brain.

When to See a Doctor

If you are reading this and either you or a loved one has suffered what you believe to be a concussion and have not yet been evaluated by a medical professional, it is very important to seek medical attention immediately! Head trauma should not be self-diagnosed and could be life threatening. In no way should this information or website be considered a substitute for a medical diagnoses or medical treatment.

Once you or your loved one is evaluated by a doctor, re-connect with us for education, real solutions, and the quickest path to recovery.

The signs and symptoms of a concussion can be trivial to diagnose and may not be immediately apparent.

IMPORTANT MESSAGE

If you are reading this and either you or a loved one has suffered what you believe to be a concussion and have not yet been evaluated by a medical professional, it is very important to seek medical attention immediately!

Head trauma should not be self-diagnosed and could be life threatening. In no way should this information or website be considered a substitute for a medical diagnoses or medical treatment. Once you or your loved one is evaluated by a doctor, re-connect with us for education, real solutions, and the quickest path to recovery.

According to the Mayo Clinic, Common symptoms after a concussive traumatic brain injury are headache, loss of memory (amnesia) or confusion. If there is amnesia, it may or may not follow a loss of consciousness, usually involves the loss of memory of the event that caused the concussion, but the memory loss may not be immediately apparent, as in the case of my son.

(In accordance with the Mayo Clinic Head Trauma Protocol Guidelines)

See a doctor if:

- You or your child experiences a head injury
- Even if emergency care isn't required The American Academy of Pediatrics recommends that you call your child's doctor for advice if your child receives anything more than a light bump on the head.
- If your child doesn't have signs of a serious head injury, and if your child remains alerted, moves normally and responds to you, the injury is probably mild and usually doesn't need further testing. In this case, if your child wants to nap, it's OK to let him or her sleep. If worrisome signs develop later, seek emergency care.

Seek emergency care for an adult or child who experiences a head injury and symptoms such as:

- Repeated vomiting
- A loss of consciousness lasting longer than 30 seconds
- A headache that gets worse over time
- Changes in his or her behavior, such as irritability
- Changes in physical coordination, such as stumbling or clumsiness
- Confusion or disorientation, such as difficulty recognizing people or places
- Slurred speech or other changes in speech

Other symptoms include:

- Seizures
- Vision or eye disturbances, such as pupils that are bigger than normal (dilated pupils) or pupils of unequal sizes
- Lasting or recurrent dizziness
- Obvious difficulty with mental function or physical coordination
- Symptoms that worsen over time
- Large head bumps or bruises on areas other than the forehead in children, especially in infants under 12 months of age

Why should you see a doctor?

The main reasons why someone should be examined after a head injury is to rule out any hemorrhaging or slow bleeding in the brain.

The hospital has a CAT scanner that can look inside the head to determine if there is any bleeding in the brain. Bleeding in the brain can be life-threatening. Blood is quite thick and heavy, and if there is enough blood in the right spot pressing down on the brain just right, it can squeeze it. These are very dangerous types of internal brain bleeding and are called epidural and subdural hematomas.

The brain is trapped inside the skull, and slow bleeding can push vital parts of the brain against the inside of the skull and through a small hole in the base of the skull called the foremen magnum. These areas of the brain are very important and control breathing and heart rate, and if squeezed, those specific areas of the brain could stop, resulting in death. Such hematomas can be surgically corrected, and there are chances for complete recovery if caught early enough.

Even if an individual hasn't passed out, no longer feels dazed and confused, and says they feel fine it is still important to have any questionable head injury evaluated by a medical professional to ensure no slow bleeding is taking place.

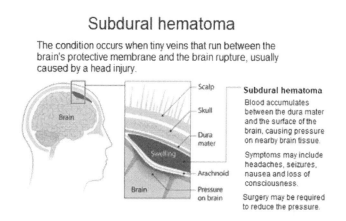

Subdural hematoma

The condition occurs when tiny veins that run between the brain's protective membrane and the brain rupture, usually caused by a head injury.

Scalp
Skull
Dura mater
Swelling
Arachnoid
Brain
Pressure on brain

Subdural hematoma

Blood accumulates between the dura mater and the surface of the brain, causing pressure on nearby brain tissue.

Symptoms may include headaches, seizures, nausea and loss of consciousness.

Surgery may be required to reduce the pressure.

Special note for athletes

No one should return to play or vigorous activity while signs or symptoms of a concussion are present. There is no game worth losing a part of yourself forever, nor does a single sport define you as much as your personality, memories, emotions and mind.

Experts recommend that an athlete with a suspected concussion not return to play until he or she has been medically evaluated by a health care professional trained in evaluating and managing concussions.

Taking the secondary injury into account, an evaluation over the following 48 hours is necessary for a complete concussion analysis.

Children and adolescents should be evaluated by a health care professional trained in evaluating and managing pediatric concussions.

Experts also recommend that adult, child and adolescent athletes with a concussion not return to play on the same day as the injury.

The risk of incurring a second concussion while still in a post-concussive state increases dramatically.

Chapter 3

The First 48 Hours after a Concussion

What you should and should not do.

The first 48 hours after a concussion are imperative, and can determine how long recovery takes and how serious the post-concussion syndrome is.

The list of what not to do far outweighs the "to do" list after a concussion and the first 24 hours are particularly crucial in concussion protocol. An aggressive approach centered on healing the brain and protecting it from further injury is the best way to ensure a quick recovery.

In this chapter, we will outline what steps should be taken and what things should be avoided within the first 24 hours to provide the best opportunity for a swift recovery.

If a concussion is not diagnosed or taken seriously, it can result in a much longer recovery time with more severe symptoms and side effects. Remember, as previously discussed in the first chapter most concussion do not reveal themselves on an MRI or CAT scan and doctors must rely on patient history and clinical observation of symptoms.

The events surrounding my son's first concussion are the best example. His concussion was not properly diagnosed; therefore, those crucial first 24 hours after the fact, when a concussion protocol plan should have been put into play, his brain did not receive proper care. I believe this was the reason for his long journey to recovery, and the severity of his post-concussion syndrome symptoms.

Warning!

Do not administer aspirin or any medications with blood thinning properties after a hit to the head as this could increase bleeding and hemorrhaging and could be fatal.

It is better not to administer any medication that you may be unfamiliar with until you see a doctor. Applying ice is the safest first step to take and can help reduce inflammation and swelling on the brain.

WARNING!

- Do not take Aspirin or medication with blood thinning properties
- This could increase risk of bleeding on the brain
- See your doctor
- Use ice do decrease inflammation on the brain

Seek medical attention

First and foremost, getting checked out by a doctor is top priority. This is to ensure there is no fracture in the skull, brain swelling, hemorrhaging, or any other medical emergencies which could be life threatening.

Seek medical attention

- ❑ Skull fractures
- ❑ Brain swelling
- ❑ Hemorrhaging
- ❑ Other life threatening emergencies

Once you have been cleared to return home, do not hesitate to call the doctor or the ER if new symptoms arise or symptoms get worse, such as:

• Headaches that get worse

• Clear drainage from the nose or ear

• Scalp swelling that gets bigger

• A seizure

• Neck pain

• Is hard to wake up

• Vomits more than once

• Cannot think clearly or remember things

• Has weakness in the arms or legs or does not move them as usual

• Cannot recognize people or places

• Slurred speech

• Passes out

• Acts differently than usual, such as if he does not play, acts fussy or seems confused or perceives to look unusual

In case of an urgent concern or emergency, call 911 or go to the nearest emergency department right away.

Complete brain rest

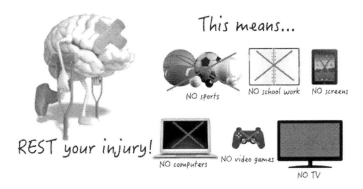

The second most important thing to do is rest, removing _ALL_ stimuli.

Just think about everything the brain is responsible for doing. The brain is a control center of the body and performs an incredible amount of tasks such as walking, talking, breathing, tasting, and regulating organ functions like that of the lungs, heart, and digestion. The brain is also responsible for other cognitive functions necessary for thinking, how to behave and learn, memories, emotions, and how we perceive the world around us.

The brain can never fully rest unless you are sleeping and even during sleep it is still functioning.

This is an ever active muscle, and like any muscle after an injury, it needs rest to heal. You wouldn't dream of walking around or running on a broken ankle, and just the same, a concussion is a brain injury so all brain exercise should be stopped!

Obviously, someone cannot stop breathing, digesting, or thinking completely, but certain things can be done to eliminate any unnecessary need for extra brain power.

In the age of information where we usually don't leave the room without mobile devices this can be a challenge; however, it cannot be just an option.

So what exactly does no stimuli look like? It looks like this:

- Lying in bed sleeping as much as possible in a dark, quiet room
- No physical activity like playing or exercise
- Low stress calm and quiet surroundings
- Abstain from thinking activities like reading, schoolwork, electronic games, talking on the phone and watching TV
- No computers, tweeting, texting, Facebooking, web surfing, listening to music, or anything similar.
- No work, no school, no sports, no activities.

In larger families, it is important for the individual recovering to be allowed ample space by themselves. Screaming babies or hyper toddlers should be kept away as much as possible.

A note for busy large families

It is important for the individual recovering to have ample time by themselves to rest.

Screaming babies, hyper toddlers or even friends and family wanting to see how they are doing are still stimuli.

I know that reducing all stimuli is not an easy task. I know, I've been there, and on a good day my home makes Grand Central station seem like a Sunday stroll; but it must be done for the brain to rest and heal. If the brain is not allowed time to heal it will result in longer concussion symptoms as well as an increase in the severity of symptoms like headaches, migraines, dizziness, fatigue and slow the healing process.

Play now = pay now and later!

During the first 24 hours, it is important to wake up a concussed individual every 3 to 4 hours during the night to evaluate if there have been any changes in symptoms. Check for signs of deteriorating mental statuses, such as the inability to gain consciousness, increased head pain, increased sense of dizziness, amnesia, or feelings of confusion. This is to rule out the possibility of any bleeding and swelling on the brain, which can be fatal, as previously discussed in Chapter 1. It is not necessary to check his eyes with a flashlight or test his reflexes. Chances are they will be very tired and want to sleep which is completely normal after a concussion.

Check for Signs od Deteriorating Mental Statuses Such as:

- Inability to gain consciousness
- Increased head pain
- Increased sense of dizziness
- Amnesia
- Feeling of confusion
- This is to rule out possibility of bleeding or swelling on the brain

Avoid extreme temperatures

It is important that someone suffering from concussion does not get exposed to extreme temperatures. Ensure the person is wearing loose clothes and he or she is resting comfortably. The mere presence of a concussion can make someone feel agitated and uncomfortable by nature, so a little TLC is necessary during this time. If the weather is either too cold or too hot, make sure the clothing is adjusted so that the body temperature does not fluctuate as this can aggravate the brain and cause further complications.

Ice packs can be used if there is swelling to help prevent further inflammation in the brain and is not considered extreme temperatures for the whole body. This rule applies more to a hot summer's day or a very cold winter's day, in which in these cases maintaining a moderate body temperature is necessary for recovery. Use adequate air-conditioning during the summer and keep a comfortable, warm temperature in the winter. During this period an individual with a concussion should not be outside walking around regardless of the temperatures, but instead, they should be sleeping and resting in bed.

This can be a difficult task with young children, as they are not often as willing to lay in bed and remain inactive. Softly, reading them a story to pass the time is the safest solution.

Implement a brain healing meal plan

The third most important thing that can be done for faster recovery is nourishing and helping to heal the brain through specific types of foods and supplements.

The Complete Concussion Protocol Nutrition Plan

- Increase protein and healthy brain fats
- See section two for complete food list
- Brain health smoothie recipe
- Brain Health Kit liquid vitamins and minerals

You can also increase recovery time by abstaining from certain foods and substances that can harm the brain like cigarettes which rob the brain of healing oxygen and alcohol which increases toxins.

Increase the daily amount of protein eaten to feed the healing brain and aid in brain muscle tissue growth. Focus on deep breaths fully oxygenating the brain. Refrain from caffeine and any other stimulants and acid type producing foods. Focus on eating an anti-inflammatory diet full of dark leafy greens to help alkaline and detox the brain environment both of which help to reduce swelling.

In section two, I will give you food lists and a complete meal plan and supplement regimen to implement throughout the concussion healing process.

As a matter of fact, not only is this type of brain healing diet beneficial for concussions, it can be implemented for anybody with neurological imbalances and for anyone who just wants to optimize their brain power and neurological health.

It is derived from the Keys2Eating how to feed your brain studies and series.

Get a head start on the healing process and order the Brain Health Liquid Vitamins and Minerals Kit here.

http://www.keys2eating.com/product/brain-health-support-kit

Be patient!

The period after concussion is a character building exercise for everyone involved not only the individual suffering from the concussion but their entire social circle.

Patience with the patient is especially important as they may become agitated and more emotional than usual. Their senses become heightened, and it will take much less to stir them up or make them feel overwhelmed.

Imagine taking a ball bat to your computer system, after a good smack; you could expect to have a few glitches.

The individual suffering with a concussion is not only suffering from physical symptoms but is also battling within. Often they don't even understand themselves why they are feeling this way, especially young children.

Emotional stress can be just as damaging as excessive stimuli.

A little extra TLC and patience can reduce recovery time, and create a closer relationship bond through the struggle.

Stay Calm

- Anxiety and stress can be high for everyone
- Emotional stress can be just as damaging as stimuli and physical stress
- Heal and grow together
- TLC can reduce recovery time and create an unforgettable bond and closer relationship

Chapter 4

What happens to the brain during a concussion?

In order to adequately treat a head injury you must understand what happens to the brain after a concussion or TBI. Furthermore, it is also necessary to understand how the brain functions on a day to day basis performing its' regular tasks. By understanding how your brain works you can put into perspective the damaging effects of the head injury and have a clearer vision of the recovery that must take place.

How the Brain Works?

Before we discuss what happens to the brain, let's create an educational foundation and first review how the brain works and the different components that help with every day brain functioning.

A critical role that the brain plays is the sending and receiving of messages throughout the brain and the body. Such messages and signals interpret information, house memories, are involved in feelings, emotions, and desires all while reminding the heart to beat and lungs to expand.

Signals and messages are sent and received inside the brain by brain cells called neurons.

Below is the picture of a neuron:

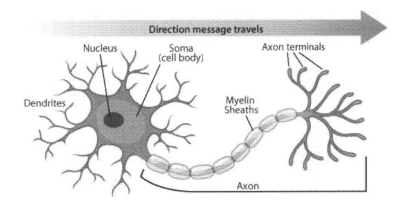

Neurons send synapses that happen like little lightning bolts from the tips of the Axons. The human brain has about 100 billion neurons.

Each neuron fires (on average) about 200 times per second, while each neuron connects to about 1,000 other neurons. This means that every time *each* neuron fires a signal action potential or synapse, 1,000 *other* neurons get that information.

How does the Brain Have an Electrical Charge and Fire?

The cell membrane separates the inside of a cell from the outside, and all chemicals that get in and out of the cell must go through it, as in the case of all cells, not just brain neurons.

The inside of the cell is negatively charged and the outside of the cell is positively charged due to specific ions (an atom or molecule with a net electric charge due to the loss or gain of one or more electrons), potassium (K+) and sodium (Na+), that move in and out of the cell.

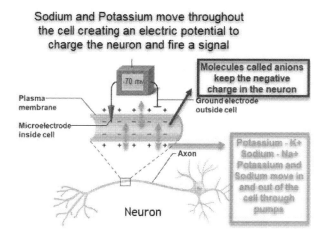

Potassium and sodium are pumped in and out of the cells through sodium-potassium pumps. They are compelled to travel because of the opposite charge that draws them near and likewise they are repelled or pushed away by a like charge.

When the inside of the neuron has a negative charge while the outside has a positive charge, it is considered to be at rest, and electrically charged across its' membrane. It has the potential to fire a message or create what's called an action potential.

To understand polarization, think of a flashlight battery. It has a + pole (the button at one end), which is positive relative to the - pole (the flat surface at the other end). Imagine that the cell membrane has lots of tiny batteries in it, with the positive button poles on the outside of the cell membrane and the flat negative pole inside, as illustrated in the figure below. This would make the inside of the cell negative relative to the outside.

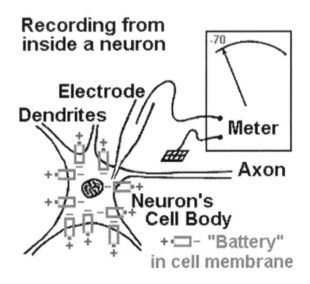

Of course, the cell membrane doesn't really have little batteries in it. The polarization is produced by chemically driven "pumps". They push positive sodium ions (Na+, atoms of sodium with a + electric charge) out of the cell, leaving behind negative ions, especially chloride ions (Cl-). The excess of negative ions left inside the cell makes it negative.

Sodium-Potassium Pumps

Extracellular   Intracellular

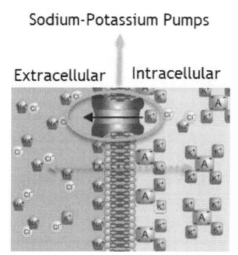

Once an action potential is sent or a signal fired, the inside of the cell becomes positive and the outside is negative. Kind of like a circuit breaker flipping. The cell must reboot or repolarize before it can fire again or before another action potential can take place.

The neuron repolarizes by turning on its sodium-potassium pumps which pump sodium out of the cell and potassium in. The pumps stay on until the proper amount of ions are on either side returning the neuron to its resting potential, negative on the inside and positive on the outside.

Once this happens the cells is repolarized and rebooted ready to fire again and perform an action potential.

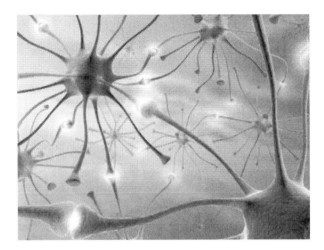

For Review:

- ✓ Neurons are nerve cells that send electrical signals along their cell membranes. At rest, (when a neuron is not sending a signal) a neuron is polarized, meaning there is an electrical charge across its cell membrane; the outside of the cell is positively charged and the inside of the cell is negatively charged.

- ✓ An electrical signal is generated when the neuron allows sodium ions to flow into it, which switches the charges on either side of the cell membrane. This switch in charge is called depolarization.

- ✓ In order to send another electrical signal, the neuron must reestablish the negative internal charge and the positive external charge. This process is called repolarization.

- ✓ A new signal cannot be sent or an action potential cannot take place until a certain electrical charge across the neuron's membrane is restored. This means the inside of the cell needs to be negative, while the outside of the cell needs to be positive.

   This process of reactivating and switching back the positive and negative charges is called repolarization.

✓ A cell repolarizes and restores itself, by turning on a protein pump in its membrane. This pump is called the sodium-potassium pump. There is a specific number and ratio of sodium and potassium pumped each time. The cell pumps two potassium ions into the cell for every three sodium ions it pumps out of the cell. The pumps do this until the proper charge inside of a cell is reached in order for it to repolarize. Once it is repolarized it can send another signal and message.

Neurons

Now that we have covered the primary function of the cells as it relates to message signaling, let's look again at the anatomy of a neuron.

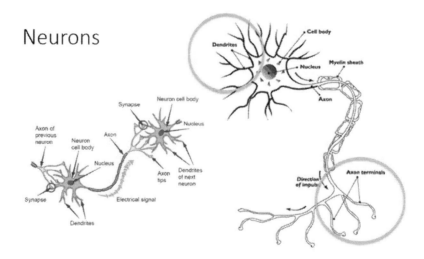

Take notice of the dendrites and axons at the opposite end of the neuron. They are very important in sending and receiving signals and messages throughout the brain. The Dendrites receive the information while the axons send the information. Both the axons and dendrites are often damaged during and after a concussion and TBI.

Chapter 5

A Concussions Silent Partner

What Most People Don't Know About Concussions

The Secondary Injury

Though each traumatic brain injury (TBI) and concussion are unique to each individual, medical science has discovered that the occurrences that follow during the secondary injury are proven to be probable and foreseeable. While the biological events occur in a very calculable fashion, the degree of damage during the secondary injury can be altered if the appropriate measures are taken.

In order to effectively be able to treat a TBI or concussion you must be aware of what takes place during the secondary injury following the initial, also called primary injury.

A multiple of very calculated sequential events occur in the brain; contributing to symptoms, or an increase in symptoms, that can continue for up to 48 hours after the initial primary injury has taken place.

There are three major events that take place effecting brain function during the secondary injury.

- ✓ Ionic shifts
- ✓ Metabolic Changes
- ✓ Impaired neurotransmission

Ionic shifts

Each healthy working brain cell maintains a resting potential energy and a charge. This is done by the cell keeping a balance between potassium (k+) inside the cell and sodium (Na+) on the outside of the cell as we discussed above. When the polarity or charge is compromised it can be referred to as depolarization.

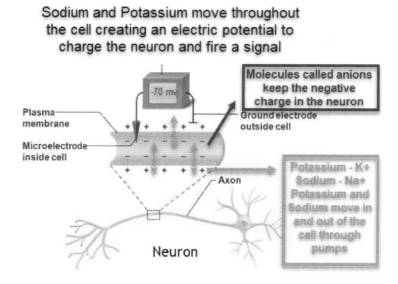

During the first few minutes after a TBI a disruption in the brain cells open up gates, allowing potassium to be released from the cells.

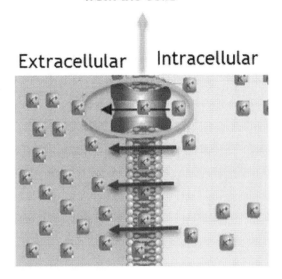

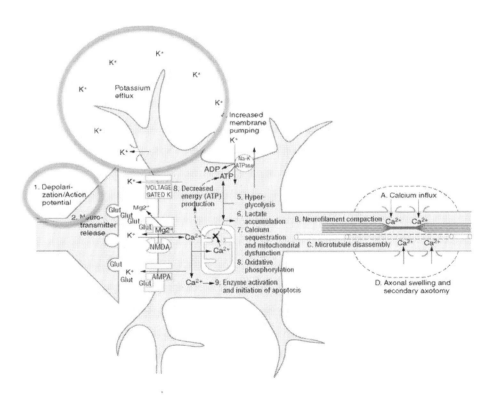

The figure above show Potassium (K+) being released around the brain cell or neuron called a Potassium efflux.

The release of potassium or efflux causes the cell to lose its balance of sodium and potassium which in turn causes the loss of polarity or resting potential energy.

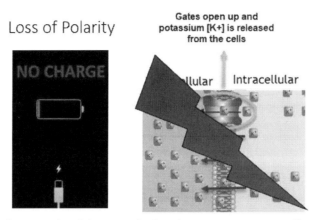

As we previously discussed, without polarity the neuron cannot fire a message and an action potential cannot take place. Therefore, stalling communication between those neurons damaged.

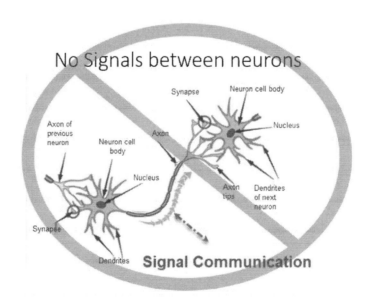

This imbalance also triggers neurotransmitters to be released around the cells. Neurotransmitters help with communication inside the cell and between other cells. The neurotransmitters effected are, glutamate (EAA), AMDA, and AMPA.

We are going to turn our focus on one neurotransmitter in specific released during this process called glutamate (EAA).

The figure below shows the neurotransmitter Glutamate being released around the cell.

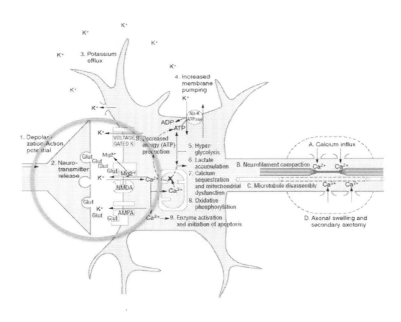

The neurotransmitter, glutamate is responsible for sending signals between the nerve cells and plays an important role in learning and memory. Too much glutamate being released in the brain can over-excite cells contributing to cellular damage and cell death.

Glutamate is responsible for sending signals between nerve cell

- Glutamate plays an important role in learning and memory

- Too much glutamate being released can over-excite cells and contribute to cell damage and death

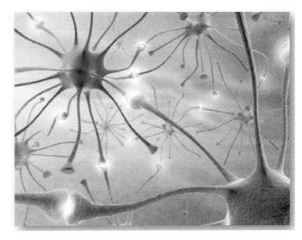

Release of neurotransmitters contributes to:

- ✓ more potassium efflux or potassium release out of cell
- ✓ sodium influx or sodium entering the cell
- ✓ Depolarizing more cells
- ✓ More cells with NO CHARGE
- ✓ Creates a domino affect

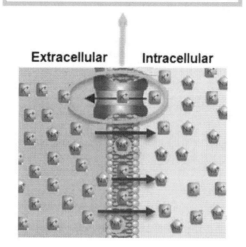

Neurotransmitter release contributes to sodium [Na+] influx or movement into cell and Potassium [K+] out of cell further

Extracellular   **Intracellular**

The release of neurotransmitters further contributes to the potassium efflux or release out of the cell and the sodium influx or movement into the cell, depolarizing more cells.

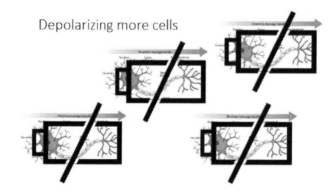

Depolarizing more cells

The brain works overtime trying to recharge and repolarize the damaged cells. In order to move potassium and sodium in and out of the cells the sodium-potassium pumps in the cell must work overtime.

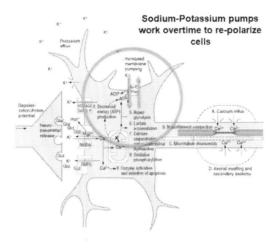

It is this excessive work load placed on the cells that creates the increase demand for more cellular food in the form of ATP (adenosine triphosphate).

This brings us to the next issue.

Metabolic changes

A quick recap, a cell repolarizes and restores itself by turning on a protein pump in its membrane. The pump is called the sodium-potassium pump. The sodium-potassium pump will not stop until the resting potential energy is restored. It is this type of relentless effort that requires the increased amounts of ATP, energy for the cell. The cell pumps in two potassium ions for every three sodium ions it pumps out. The pumps do this until the proper charge inside of a cell is reached in order for it to repolarize. Once it is repolarized it can send another signal and message.

Quick Re-Cap (after all this is brain science)

- Requires a lot of energy and ATP
- Cell pumps in 2 potassium [K+] ions for every 3 sodium [Na+] ion it pumps out
- The pumps do this until the proper charge is reached in order for it to repolarize

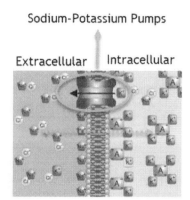

Sodium-Potassium Pumps

Extracellular | Intracellular

During the initial stages of the secondary injury the brain is working overtime to repolarize and recharge the depolarized cells. The increased work load placed on the cells creates a demand for more cellular energy.

Secondary injury initial stages

- The brain is working overtime to repolarize and recharge the depolarized or dead cells
- The increased work load creates a demand for more cellular energy.

The cell uses energy in the form of ATP (adenosine triphosphate) and creates it by using or metabolizing glucose (sugar). Because the cells are working so hard to recharge and repolarize the cells they need an increased amount of ATP or energy.

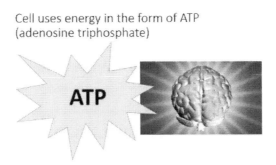

To accommodate for this increased demand of ATP the brain initiates an elevation in glucose metabolism. However, because of the damage done to the cells and their inability to work efficiently the glucose production cannot keep up with the glucose demands so a glucose metabolic depression occurs.

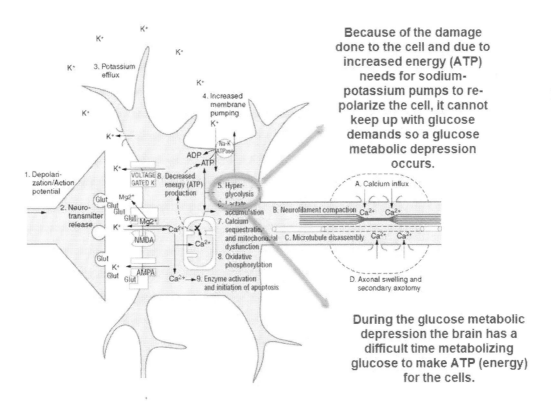

During a glucose metabolic depression the brain has a difficult time metabolizing glucose in order to make ATP (energy) for the cells.

Glucose Metabolic Depression

- Sodium-potassium pumps use up glucose
- Glucose uptake and production cannot keep up with demand
- Glucose metabolic depression occurs
- Cell energy ATP cannot be produced
- Cells die

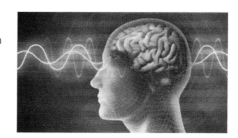

Problems metabolizing glucose to produce ATP for cells during a time when the brain is requiring extra energy supply to reestablish the homeostasis within the cells, is not conducive to recovery.

What does this mean for concussed person?

- Increase in number and intensity of symptoms
- Longer recovery time

This metabolic depression and fuel shortage contributes to more depolarization, increased cellular behavior dysfunction, and cell death.

This increase in glucose demand occurs immediately following a concussion or TBI

Problems metabolizing glucose

- Very bad at a time when demand is high
- Cells do not have enough energy or ATP
- Sodium-Potassium pumps cannot continue to pump
- Brain cells (neurons) cannot repolarize
- Cell cannot send or receive messages to and from other cells
- Eventually cell dies

The result is permanent death of the brain cell

and can continue up to four hours depending on the degree of the concussion or TBI. After this period the brain falls into a glucose metabolic depression.

Increased Glucose Demand

- Occurs immediately following the initial head injury
- Can last up to 4 hours following a concussion or TBI
- Leaves the cell in a glucose metabolic depression

Oxidative Metabolism

One contributor to the glucose metabolic depression is the impairment of oxidative metabolism due to damage in the brain.

Oxidative metabolism is a chemical process in which oxygen is used to make energy from carbohydrates (sugars). It's kind of like oxygen being one of the ingredients in the recipe to make energy or ATP. Oxidative metabolism has a few names and is also called aerobic metabolism, aerobic respiration, and cell respiration.

Oxidative Metabolism

- A chemical process
- Oxygen is needed and used to make energy from carbohydrates (sugars)
- Aerobic metabolism
- Aerobic respiration
- Cell respiration

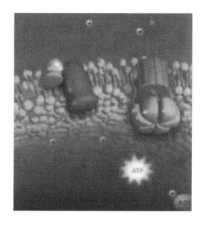

All of these contributing factors make it more difficult to utilize glucose (sugar) as the primary fuel for the cells energy production in the form of ATP.

It is based on this research and evidence that we incorporate different means for the brain cells to obtain energy other than glucose in our concussion protocol meal plan.

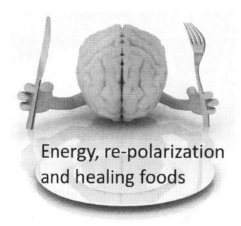

Energy, re-polarization and healing foods

Finding other ways for the brain cells and neurons to obtain the ATP and energy they need to survive and reach homeostasis avoids the metabolic depression and negative effects that come with it.

Research shows that by providing the cells with the increase in fuel necessary to recharge and reach homeostasis, you can decrease recovery time and lesson the amount of damage done by the secondary injury.

All of this adds up to fewer concussion symptoms and reduced recovery time.

We will cover in detail this alternate form of energy for the cell and how to obtain it in section two, The Concussion Protocol Meal Plan.

Impaired neurotransmission

Within the brain there are over 100 billion nerve cells called neurons sending electrical and chemical messages through the body.

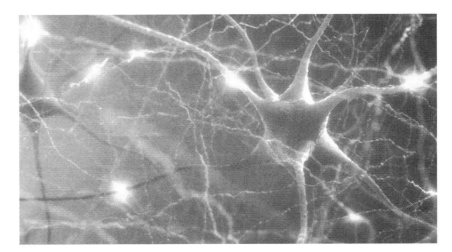

Each neuron has a cell body, a long nerve fiber called an axon in projections of the cell bodies called dendrites. Dendrites stick out from the cell body to see signals from surrounding neurons.

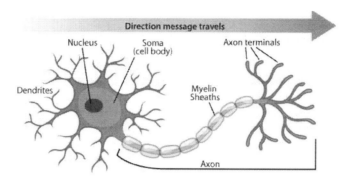

Axons connect neurons to each other sending messages throughout the brain.

Each neurons fires (on average) about 200 times per second, while each neuron

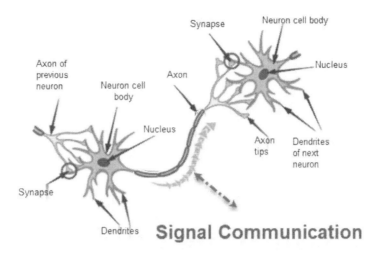

connects to about 1,000 other neurons. The picture below is a representation of the incredible constant firing of neurons in the brain. If you could only imagine the largest and most powerful computer processor located in your head.

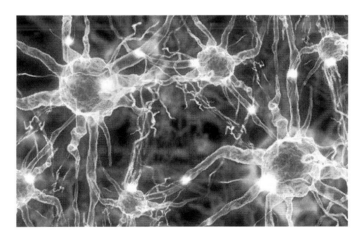

This means that every time *each* neuron fires a signal action potential or synapse, 1,000 *other* neurons get that information.

Now we can do the math, let's multiply:

    100 billion neurons

X

    200 firings per second

X

    1,000 connections each

Answer: 20,000,000,000,000,000 bits of info transmitted per second

Just try to interpret that number: 20 million billion bits of information move around your brain every second.

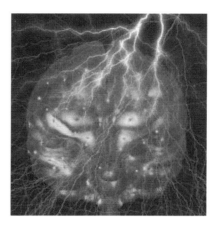

Can you imagine what would happen if that communication system was on the fritz?

When the brain bounces back and forth inside the skull during a TBI or concussion areas of the brain slide over each other at different speeds. Axons across these areas stretch, tear and break off from the cell body.

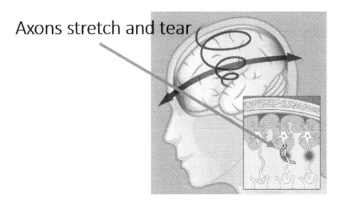

This is called axonal shearing or diffuse axonal injury, DAI.

Damage to the axons can lead to a breakdown of communication among neurons in the brain.

Brain damage can continue to occur for hours and even days after the initial injury.

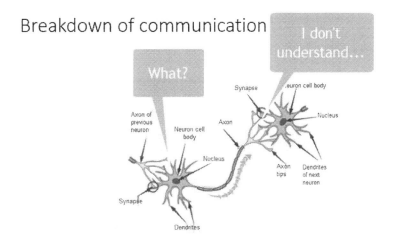

Diffuse axonal injury and axonal shearing

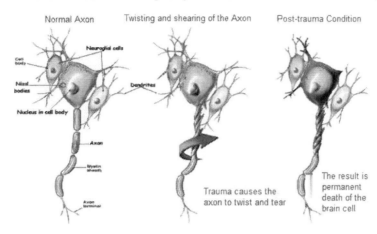

The torn axons quickly degenerate releasing toxic levels of chemicals called neurotransmitters into the extracellular space.

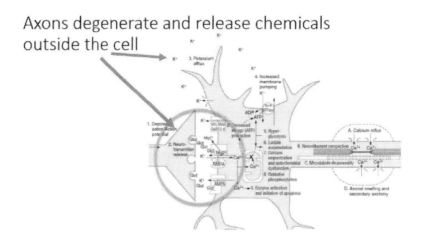

The release of these neurotransmitters causes many of the surrounding neurons to die over the next 24 to 48 hours worsening the initial effects of the injury and contributing to post-concussion symptoms.

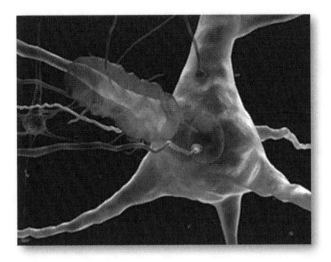

Symptoms of mild to moderate diffuse axonal injury (DAI), like those found in concussions are; brief loss of consciousness, impaired long-term memory, reduced problem-solving ability, lower social inhibition, and attention and perception problems.

Symptoms of disuse axonal shearing

- Brief loss of consciousness (not necessary)
- Impaired long-term memory
- Reduced problem solving ability
- Lower social inhibition
- Attention and perception problems

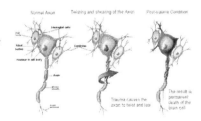

Mild TBI's or concussions are typically not visible by CT and MRI. The doctors must rely on patient history and a clinical exam to make a diagnosis.

It is crucial to understand what takes place during the secondary injury to ensure the proper concussion treatment is given.

A neuro-metabolic study concluded that post injury metabolic conditions did not correlate closely with the severity of the TBI as measured on the Glasgow Score. This means that even people who did not test high with concussion symptoms still suffered from this secondary injury.

The Secondary Injury

- Research shows that severity of concussion isn't necessarily connected to level of the secondary injury

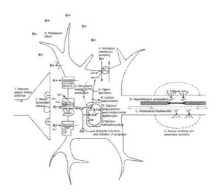

Also, depressed glucose metabolism was seen in comatose patients as well as in walking, talking patients. This suggests that significant metabolic problems and abnormalities may occur even without serious clinical symptoms.

Depressed glucose metabolism

Depressed glucose metabolism was seen in all levels of patients. Those comatose, as well as, walking, talking and even without serious clinical symptoms.

This being said, when treating or responding to a concussion, even what might seem like a mild concussion should be taken seriously and treated completely by following all protocol steps, including and not limited to The Concussion Protocol Meal Plan.

If the treatment of a concussion is contingent only upon the initial evaluation immediately following the injury, omitting ongoing analysis over the following 48 hours, the person suffering may receive inadequate care and needlessly suffer from upcoming symptoms unbeknownst to them and others.

IMPORTANT!

If the treatment of a concussion is contingent only upon the initial evaluation immediately following the injury, omitting ongoing analysis over the following 48 hours, the person suffering may receive inadequate care and needlessly suffer from upcoming symptoms unbeknownst to them and others.

Chapter 6

Concussion Evaluation and Medical Tests

What you can expect and request

Pre-Concussion Tests

Baseline testing is a pre-season exam conducted by a trained health care professional. Baseline tests are used to assess an athlete's balance and brain function as well as the presence of any concussion symptoms. Results from baseline tests (or pre-injury tests) can be used and compared to a similar exam conducted by a health care professional during the season if an athlete has a suspected concussion.

Baseline testing has become very common before athletic seasons especially in football. If your athlete's sports teams are not utilizing baseline concussion testing, I urge you to request a baseline test for your athlete or yourself and educate the coaches on the fact that no athlete in any sport is immune to a concussion. Education and exposure is a key factor in concussion prevention. You can simply search, "baseline testing" on the internet and locate centers near you.

Pre Concussion Tests

Baseline Test

- Pre season exam
- Performed on a computer
- When taken after injury test results are compared with initial pre-season test results to determine reaction time differences
- Offered in most cities and can be requested

Impact and Baseline Testing

Concussion Screenings and Tests

As previously discussed one of the imminent dangers a concussion can bring is swelling on the brain, neurological glitches that can cause seizures, fractures in the skull upon impact and brain tissue damage.

The test performed in the ER or physician's office is geared towards detecting these complications and more.

Most concussion screening tests are not invasive and are painless. If the test results show a sufficient amount of swelling or surgery is needed, the patient will be administered anesthesia, and the doctor will explain the procedures and diagnoses.

The following are some standard concussion screening tests the patient can expect to undergo during their evaluation after the diagnoses of a possible concussion:

CT Scan - A special computerized x-ray that provides images of the brain and is used to look for suspected hydrocephalus, fluid build-up in the brain which causes the brain to swell

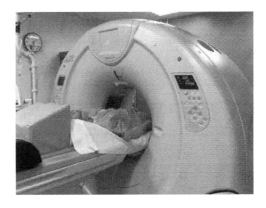

MRI Scan - Provides detailed images of the brain using magnetic energy rather than radiation which is used in regular x-rays.

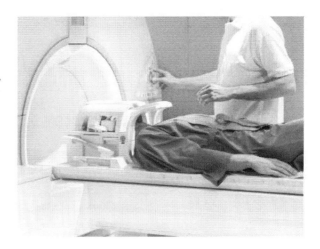

X-Rays - Internal images of the body that are best for seeing fractures in bones and to look at the lungs when pneumonia is suspected. X-rays do not hurt but do involve a small amount of radiation.

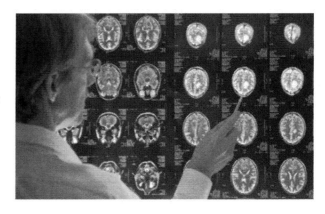

Evoked Potential - Assesses the ability of nerves to send information from the body to the brain and is used to measure visual, hearing and sensory function, most often in minimally responsive patients who are unable to participate in a regular physical exam.

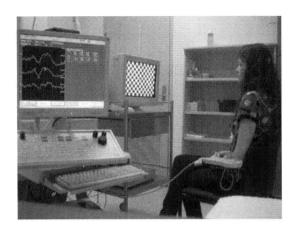

EEG (electroencephalogram) – records the electrical activity of the brain and can sometimes help predict risk for seizures. It does not hurt, but it does require the use of a medical adhesive that may cause discomfort when removed from the hair.

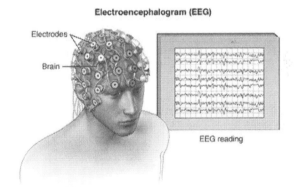

Electroencephalogram (EEG)

Electrodes

Brain

EEG reading

EMG/NCV (electromyogram and nerve conduction studies) – records the electrical activity of muscles and nerves. It is also used to predict risk for seizures, and like an EEG, it does not hurt, but it does require the use of a medical adhesive that may cause discomfort when removed from the hair.

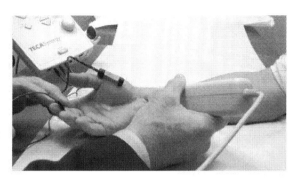

The diagnosis of a concussion and/or brain injury involves looking for signs of brain injury, either through scanning devices like computer assisted tomography (CAT scans), magnetic resonance imaging (MRIs), and X-rays, or through screening tools, usually in the form of simple tests, that measure various areas of a person's speech, movement, memory, and thought.

The people most qualified to diagnose a brain injury are emergency room doctors, neurologists, and neuropsychologists.

Chapter 7

How to identify and how to prepare for

Post-Concussion Syndrome.

As a mother, with a son who has suffered three concussions to date, one being severe; I have seen the behind the scenes of someone struggling with post-concussion syndrome, the disbelief from others and the feelings they carry of being misunderstood.

In the first few hours and days after a concussion, it is common to experience some dizziness, poor concentration and other symptoms. These symptoms can even worsen due to the secondary injury, and metabolic cascade that follows the primary injury which is covered in detail in chapter 5.

Post-concussion syndrome is a complex disorder in which various symptoms such as headaches and dizziness last for weeks and sometimes months after the injury that caused the concussion.

In my son's case, it took a complete year before all of the post-concussion syndrome symptoms were gone after his first concussion.

Post-concussion syndrome, like concussions, can be unique in nature. The initial injury from the concussion like bruising, swelling, ionic disturbances, metabolic changes, transmission interruptions, and injury to the brain will heal then sometimes the patient develops post-concussion syndrome.

What is Post-Concussion Syndrome?

- A complex syndrome and disorder
- Symptoms like headaches, dizziness, mood disturbances
- Duration can last from day, to months or even longer

Doctors cannot initially detect which concussion patients may or may not develop post-concussion syndrome, but one way to reduce the probability and severity of post-concussion syndrome is to implement a concussion protocol system within the first 24 hours and rest the brain.

Post-concussion syndrome is an entirely separate ailment following a concussion and traumatic brain injury (TBI) that can bring its own set of symptoms and issues.

A character trait of post-concussion syndrome is that symptoms continue longer than would be expected from the nature of the injury, and often get worse over time. Whereas,

When does someone develop Post Concussion Syndrome?

- After the bruising, swelling, and initial injury heals
- Once the secondary Impact from ionic disturbances, metabolic changes and transmission interruptions are gone
- Some are left with an entirely new disorder to overcome

symptoms directly related to the head injury are worst at the beginning and slowly improve.

How do I know if it is Post Concussion Syndrome?

- Symptoms continue longer than would be expected from the nature of the injury
- Symptoms can get worse over time instead of better

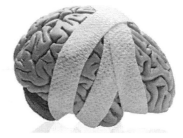

Some experts believe post-concussion symptoms are caused by structural damage to the brain or disruption of neurotransmitter systems, resulting from the impact that caused the concussion.

Others believe post-concussion symptoms are related to psychological factors, especially since the most common symptoms are a headache, dizziness and sleep problems which are similar to those often experienced by people diagnosed with depression, anxiety or post-traumatic stress disorder.

Why does Post Concussion Syndrome develop?

- Some medical research suggests it's caused by structural damage to the brain or disruption of neurotransmitter systems
- Others believe symptoms are related to psychological factors since most common symptoms are headache, dizziness, sleep problems, depression, anxiety and post traumatic stress disorder (PTSD) similarities

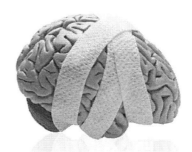

In many cases, both physiological effects of brain trauma, emotional reactions to these effects, and how the healing process was handled play a role in the development of symptoms.

3 influences in Post Concussion Syndrome

- Physiological effects of the brain trauma
- Emotional reactions the effects of the brain trauma
- How the healing process was handled

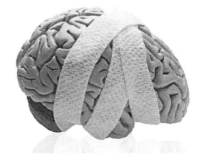

Researchers haven't determined why some people develop persistent post-concussion syndrome and others do not. There is also no proven connection between the severity of the injury and the likelihood of developing persistent post-concussion syndrome symptoms.

Who will get Post Concussion Syndrome?

- Researchers haven't determined why some concussed individuals develop post-concussion syndrome and others do not
- No connection between severity of injury and the development of post-concussion syndrome

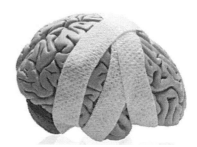

Sometimes, there can be a lull of symptoms between a concussion and the onset of post-concussion syndrome. This can often make people feel discouraged as post-concussive syndrome can be seen as a major setback in the recovery process.

Regardless of why post-concussion syndrome occurs is irrelevant and does not change the fact that it can be a long and challenging journey.

It is essential to understand and expect the possibility of the onset of post-concussion syndrome to be prepared and not caught off guard.

Mysteries of Post Concussion Syndrome?

- There can be a lull of symptoms between a concussion and post concussion syndrome
- The new or re-development of symptomatic conditions can be discouraging and seen as a set back in recovery

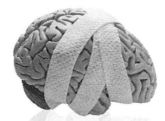

If there is not a clear separation in time between symptoms, it can appear as though the concussion injury is causing the increase in severity of symptoms, so it is important to know the difference between the initial injury concussion symptoms and concussion syndrome symptoms.

It can help to keep a log or journal during the initial days and even weeks following a concussion to have a clear understanding of symptoms. You can also use a digital voice recorder on your phone if you do not want to journal or write because of concussion symptoms.

Some Tips to Help

- It may not always be clear whether it is the initial concussion injury or post-concussion syndrome
- Journaling symptoms audibly or vlogging is better to avoid excess stimuli during recovery
- Incorporating the symptom tracker provided in the third section of this program can help better define where the concussed individual may be in the recovery journey

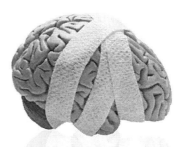

There is a concussion symptom log located in the third section of this book along with a link so you can download as many copies as necessary for the duration of recovery.

Usually, after the first 48 hours no new bleeding on the brain or swelling will occur, so a slight increase or appearance of certain symptoms listed below could be the result of the secondary injury due to damage to the neurons, brain cells, or the onset of post-concussion syndrome.

If there are ever any concerns, it is always best to call the ER or check with your doctor to make sure everything is okay. Peace of mind can be a strong medicine.

Post-concussion syndrome symptoms

Post-concussion symptoms include:

- Headaches
- Dizziness
- Fatigue
- Irritability
- Anxiety
- Insomnia
- Loss of concentration and memory
- Noise and light sensitivity

Headaches that occur after a concussion can vary and may feel like tension-type headaches or migraines. Most, however, are tension-type headaches, which may be associated with a neck injury that happened at the same time as the head injury. For instance, in a whip lash like movement during a car accident resulting in a Coup Contrecoup injury.

Dizziness can be caused by a knock to the head of any sort can dislodge 'grit' in the balance parts of the ear which is called benign paroxysmal positional vertigo (BPPV)). There can be no particular reason found for symptoms and tests such as MRI brain scanning are normal.

People often experience behavior or emotional changes after concussions and during post concussive syndrome. Others may notice that the person has become more irritable, suspicious, argumentative or stubborn.

It is during this tsunami that a wave of symptoms can arise, and it seems as though recovery begins to take a major setback.

By remembering that the first 48 hours are crucial in reducing the impact of post concussive syndrome, an implementing a concussion protocol system you can reduce the risk of a long post-concussive syndrome recovery. I believe my son's first concussion experience was so severe and recovery time took so long due to the fact no concussion plan was put into play, and we missed that initial window critical for proper healing.

Remember!

- The first 48 matter!
- Implement the concussion protocol to help reduce the risk of long term post concussion recovery

Post concussive syndrome is a very legitimate ailment that can sometimes come with debilitating symptoms. As these symptoms persist and time goes by, others can unintentionally lose compassion and empathy. Patience, support, and endurance of those around the individual suffering from post-concussive syndrome are needed for complete recovery.

Though neurologists, psychiatrists, and medical doctors can prescribe prescription medications to try and help reduce post concussive syndrome symptoms, you can choose natural remedies to help heal, and detox the brain. Neurological drugs also have side effects and can alter the body's natural production of chemicals, making them difficult to get off of.

Some of the key neurological, psychiatric drugs on the market are very damaging to vital organs like your liver. When possible, it is best to heal the body without sacrificing other areas of the body. Help your body heal while focusing on complete and total wellness.

Psychiatric Medications and Post-Concussion Syndrome
A Personal Story

I would like to go back to my son's story and tell you a personal experience we had during his walk through post concussive syndrome.

Unfortunately, many people, including myself, did not understand this after-math of a concussion and it was a long, difficult journey. After initially being cleared from his concussion, the dizziness, ringing in the ears (tinnitus), and headaches became so severe they would be completely debilitating at times. It was all he could do to sit up and the light sensitivity was so extreme that he just wanted to lay in a dark room.

It was heart breaking for me to see him like this and I was forced to watch as he became more and more dejected just wanting to return to his normal self.

During this time the school believed he appeared to be fine because he didn't have any visible injuries on the outside. They began to project an attitude of disbelief and disregard for his condition and the continued symptoms.

After time went by with these continued symptoms his neurologist and concussion specialist suggested he be seen. We made the two hour commute and he was admitted into the hospital for concussion evaluation and treatment.

I remember we both felt so relieved expecting to find this amazing cure that would return him to the physically active boy he used to be.

In efforts to reduce his headaches the doctors administered an anti-epileptic drug called Depakote (valproic acid) via IV. Depakote is a common drug used to treat migraines, seizures, and mood disorders in children and adults.

Initially, I wasn't concerned and trusted the doctors, after all up to this point it had been al misery. I just wanted him to have some relief.

After the first hour of receiving the drug he began to say that he was having a difficult time moving his legs. I thought maybe he just needed to stretch and move about a bit. He hung his legs over the side of the bed struggling and stood up very slowly. He looked as though he was balancing on wobbly stilts.

I asked him if he was ok and he said his legs felt like they were too small for his body.

I thought that was odd and we contacted the nurse to discuss this with the doctor.

They didn't seem concerned and continued administering the Depakote via IV. At about 2 ½ hours into the treatment he got up to try and use the bathroom but his legs buckled underneath him and he reach out to the IV pole to catch himself. I offered my assistance but he assertively told me he could do it himself. His frustration yet persistence was very evident so I stepped back. He was not used to having to depend on so much help and did not like it at all. He proceeded to the bathroom holding onto the pole dragging his legs across the floor. I alerted the nurse again regarding the increase in the lack of mobility to his legs but they continued the Depakote drip without concern.

After 6 hours of treatment, he lost complete mobility in his legs and couldn't even stand by himself. His description of the feeling was consistent and he said that he felt like he had little legs and they couldn't hold up his body.

I was done at this point and had the nurses call his neurologist to discontinue the treatment. The neurologists insisted to me this was not the result of the drugs, as they had not come across such a reaction before.

As any mama bear might do, I completed research through the night on this drug and came across a girl my son's age who had a similar "drunken like response" as it was explained, when given the same dose of Depakote through an IV.

The next morning he still had no mobility in his legs, and his emotional state was declining rapidly, and after enough persistence, they granted me my wish and took him off of the Depakote. It was unfortunate that it was not done without a degree of condescending treatment.

Almost to the minute of the initial dosage, within 6 hours of stopping the medication, he could walk again.

During this time not only did he lose the use of his legs but he also experienced negative psychological effects from the drug and became very depressed and anxious.

After this situation I saw the frustration and sadness in my son's eyes. He wasn't getting better, his teachers didn't believe him the medicine the doctors gave him didn't work and even they questioned the validity of his loss of mobility. I seemed to be the only one who knew him and was with him around the clock to notice the truth.

When he asked me what we were going to do I could not let him down and there was no way I was going to tell him we were out of options. I knew that I must find another option. It was at this place in our concussion journey that The Complete Concussion Protocol was be created.

I know that everyone's situation is different; however, based on our position it was our choice to continue treatment without the use of psychiatric type medications and neurological drugs.

Treatment Options

It was at this stage of my son's concussion that we began to aggressively implement this natural approach to help his brain heal.

In the second section you will be given in detail the concussion protocol nutritional guidelines, education and meal plan along with complimenting meditation and reconstruction exercises.

Treatment Options

- Medical and psychiatric drugs
- Meditation and mind calming techniques
- Natural remedies including food choices and vitamins without the risk of side effects

I will not be covering medication nor is any of this information meant to be taken as medical advice. This is intended for informational purposes only and you should discuss implementing any program with your doctor. I am going to show you the approach that I took with my son as another option, other than psychiatric medications and teach you how to implement this plan aiding the brain through the recovery process through the use of foods, vitamins, minerals, meditation and re-constructional techniques.

The beauty of using the concept of food and a natural approach is that it removes the harmful elements like the possibility of dependency and the side effects like the ones that we experienced with neurological drugs.

Much research has been done to date showing the direct connection that certain foods can have on the brain. For example, Insulin resistance, obesity, and glucose metabolic issues have all been linked to the development of Alzheimer's, dementia, memory, mood disorders, headaches, and depression.

Reducing blood glucose levels and balancing insulin levels can be a very effective way to positively influence and reduce psychological symptoms associated with post-concussion syndrome without the use of psychiatric or neurological drugs.

Food and diet directly effects brain health

Reducing blood glucose levels and balancing insulin levels to *reduce psychological symptoms associated with post-concussion syndrome without the use of psychiatric or neurological drugs.*

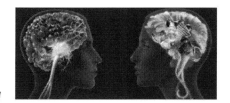

In addition to regulating blood sugar levels, increasing healthy fats is another way to help aid the brain in the recovery process.

Incorporating a modified ketogenic diet is very effective way to stabilize blood sugar levels, increase ATP or fuel for the brain and regulate brain neurotransmitters is by incorporating a modified ketogenic diet.

A modified ketogenic diet is a meal plan that focuses on increasing fat intake on a regular basis. In the upcoming chapters you will be taught a specific type of ketogenic diet that focuses on increasing quality healthy fats in efforts to regulate blood sugar levels, offer an alternative energy (ATP) supply through the production of ketones, help the brain achieve polarity within the cells in order to reach homeostasis, and stabilize major neurotransmitter production.

Ketogenic diet and brain health

- Regulate blood sugar levels
- Offer an alternative energy supply through the production of ketones
- Increases the ability to achieve polarity within the cells in order to reach homeostasis
- Stabilize major neurotransmitter production within the brain

Introduction to ketosis

Since the beginning of time, man has been equipped to survive. The body has an amazing mechanism which kept the human race alive during times of famine. This mechanism is the ability to burn body fat and metabolize fat turning it into fuel.

In normal metabolism, carbohydrates are converted into glucose and used to

- Natural mechanism
- Kept the human race alive through times of famine
- The body's ability to convert fat into ketones to use as fuel instead of carbohydrates and glucose

provide energy for the body. Cells in the body use energy in the form of ATP. Under some circumstances, like in fasting, glucose is not available because the person is not eating enough carbohydrates to convert into glucose to meet the metabolic and caloric needs for the body.

When this happens, for survival, the liver converts or breaks down fat into fatty acids and ketone bodies that provide an alternate source of fuel for energy production to the entire body including the brain.

In the absence of carbohydrates and glucose

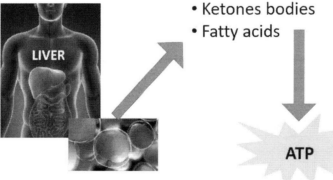

- Ketones bodies
- Fatty acids

ATP

To sum it up, when you don't eat enough carbohydrates to produce energy for your body, your liver will use your fat storage and break it down into fatty acids and ketones to use for energy.

This is why ketogenic diets are so effective for weight loss. The reason a modified ketogenic diet is used in the Concussion Protocol is to encourage the body to create ketones because of the benefit that they have on the brain specifically as it relates to concussion recovery. We are going to focus more on ketogenic and modified ketogenic diets in the next chapter.

An alternate form of energy for the brain to use other than glucose is ketones. Through a ketogenic diet you can reduce blood glucose levels, regulate insulin levels, and obtain specific benefits of increasing healthy fats.

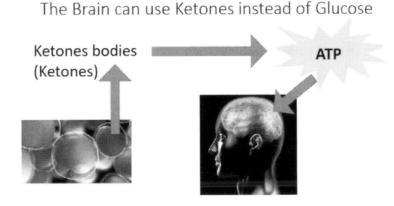

Regulating insulin levels, lowering blood sugar levels and increasing healthy fats helps to reduce and possibly avoid unwanted post-concussion syndrome symptoms.

Ketogenic Meal Plans

- Regulates insulin levels
- Lowers blood sugar levels
- Increases healthy fats for brain health
- Helps to reduce and possibly avoid unwanted post-concussion syndrome symptoms.

Section Two

"How to feed the brain"

How to eat to help the brain heal after a concussion, including a complete meal plan with recipes

Chapter 8

How to help your brain heal through foods

I want to begin this chapter with a very passionate message. I believe there is a place for modern medicine. Our doctors and neurologists today should be valued, as these are the men and women we turn to during a life-threatening emergencies trusting them with our lives and the lives of our children.

There have been countless research experiments by medical doctors and scientists

in efforts

to understand the brain and the impact that TBI and concussions have on the brain.

Without these researchers, their medical findings, and medical science, we would not have the information we do today and our treatment methods and options would be lacking.

I have had the opportunity to interview and work with some of these renowned specialists who give so much of themselves in efforts to increase awareness of TBI and concussion as they work effortlessly desiring to give the best care to their patients.

My focus in this chapter is not to take away from medical science, but rather to assist in its efforts by providing you with additions in the options of therapeutic care and steps you can do to best aid the brain during its journey towards complete recovery without the need of extra medications.

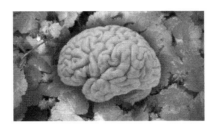

I believe in the balance of health. Certain conditions require medications to be administered, but there may be other instances when the use of medications can be avoided by addressing certain health issues.

For example, specific types of diabetes require insulin dosing. However, in the case of type 2 diabetes, which accounts for almost 90% of diabetes cases, the development of insulin resistance is mostly due to a consistent diet high in sugars and processed foods.

Type 2 Diabetes

- About 90% of diabetes cases
- Insulin Resistance
- Develops over time
- Brought on by diet and lifestyle

In the scenario of many type 2 diabetes cases, a change in health habits, surrounding diet and food choices could have helped many of these individuals avoid the need for insulin and other medications.

Another example, is heart disease. The first stage of heart disease is inflammation in the arteries, and there are certain food groups and food types that can contribute to more inflammation, as well as other food alternatives that contain anti-inflammatory properties, helping to reduce inflammation in the body.

The first tests for heart disease used to begin with the testing of cholesterol levels, but now many doctors are instituting cutting edge new methods to check first for the presence of inflammation.

All that being said, wouldn't it be a better option to reduce inflammation through diet and better health, lowering your chances of heart disease and avoid needing to take medication for heart disease all together?

Heart Disease

- Begins with inflammation in the arteries and the body
- Processed and sugar filled foods increase inflammation
- Greens, detoxing and alkalizing foods decrease inflammation

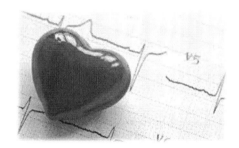

It is this type of preventative and assertive approach we will be taking when discussing brain health after a concussion or TBI.

I must give one more disclaimer here, if you or the concussed individual has been prescribed medication by a doctor, DO NOT DISCONTINUE THE MEDICATION. You could put yourself or the concussed individual in danger. Rather review with the

IMPORTANT MESSAGE

Do not discontinue any doctor ordered prescriptions especially neurological medications before talking with your doctor.

Some neurological medications cannot be stopped without dosing measurements and could result in major health complications like seizures.

attending physician the additional complimentary options and benefits that introducing a brain health meal plan offers.

Fortunately, everything you are going to learn can be beneficial even if you are taking medication.

Also, the benefits of incorporating the natural healing factors of food and nutrition are that there are no contraindications, meaning they will not interfere with or cause danger when mixed with medications.

Benefits of Incorporating a Health Meal Plan

- No contraindications with meds
- No negative side effects
- Many powerful healing properties

One exception is with certain anti-seizure medications often used in concussion treatment, citrus fruit, specifically grapefruit can interfere with release and absorption amounts.

Do Not Mix:

Seizure medications

Always read any warning labels on medications and thoroughly discuss all prescriptions with a physician and the pharmacist. Neurological medications should never be taken lightly.

Remember to review and discuss any of the complete concussion protocol steps you are implementing with your doctor during your follow-up visits. It is good for your doctor to be aware of your participation in your health care.

Your Concussion Protocol

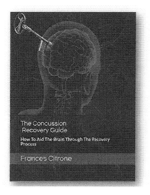 

In this next section, you will learn what foods are especially good at nourishing the brain, the necessary amounts to consume, and what vitamins and minerals the brain needs for sustained neurological health.

You will have food recipes like a powerful brain support smoothie that not only tastes great but is a perfect start to every day for everyone.

Included

- Food recipes
- Food lists
- Nutritional training
- Brain health vitamins and minerals

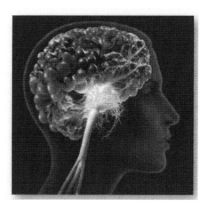

The fundamentals of this health plan, are the foundation of the Keys2Eating, How to Feed Your Brain Series.

The Keys2Eating program targets specific health concerns and uses natural foods, vitamins, and supplements to aid the brain through the extensive recovery process. In this case, our target focus is healing the brain and obtaining high functioning neurological performance.

 **Keys2Eating**

- Specific health concerns
- Use natural foods, vitamins, and supplements as a treatment option
- Aid the brain in recovery
- Obtain high functioning neurological performance

This program was developed after the experience I had with my son. When neurological drugs had left him unable to walk, I needed another option to help treat his symptoms. I needed to put together a complete health program, since the only option offered to us and often the only choice given for post-concussion syndrome is the use of psychiatric and other neurological drugs.

By learning and implementing the concepts into a daily health plan, my son and others have noticed an improvement in clarity, concentration, and mood. As a bonus, people often experience an improvement in entire physical body health.

By Implementing This Program

- Clarity
- Concentration
- Mood
- Improvement in total body health

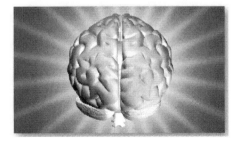

You will also discover that this health approach towards eating offers some extra benefits, and can also help burn unwanted fat, lower and eliminate inflammation in the body, sculpt muscle and offer incredible strength and endurance.

I know that sounds like a big promise; however, not only does this information come from proven research, but I have personally implemented this program in the lives of my entire family.

Not only did my son recover fully from three concussions and is currently performing well in school, free from chronic headaches and emotional fatigue, my mental clarity and health have never been better, my daughter's sleep apnea and focus issues have disappeared, and my husband lost over 80 pounds at age 46 without exercise. I know it works!

My Husband

Before

After

The brain's nutritional needs

In order for you to understand why specific elements are incorporated into The Complete Concussion Protocol, I want to first start with discussing the brain's nutritional needs. The brain is the control center of the body and performs an incredible amount of tasks such as walking, talking, breathing, tasting, and regulating organ functions like that of the lungs, heart, and digestion. The brain is also responsible for other cognitive functions necessary

for thinking, how we behave and learn, memories, emotions, and how we perceive the world around us.

This complex computing device has proven to be so fast that the most powerful computers in the world cannot emulate its processing speed. In 2014 a group of computer researchers from Japan and Germany was able to simulate 1 second of brain activity. However, it took 40 minutes and the use of 82,944 processors.

The brain requires very specific nutrients, vitamins, and minerals to do its' job efficiently and effectively. A high-performance machine like that must be well cared for, or else quality performance can be altered. Brain health suffers when deprived of necessary vital nutrients, and cognitive impairment begins.

The brain uses the greatest percentage of nutrients consumed, more than any other organ. Cognitive function demands 20% of all glucose broken down, 35% of all vitamins and minerals, 40% of all water, and a staggering 50% of fats. Which can be expected when that particular organ is organizing everything!

% of Nutrients Consumed by the Brain

- 20% of all glucose broken down
- 35% of all vitamins and minerals
- 40% of all water
- 50% of all fats

Foods that are particularly good at nourishing our brains are the ones that have high amounts of fats, nutrients, water, and just a little carbohydrates (or glucose). Your brain requires the same nutrients that every cell in your body needs. It demands macronutrients like fat, protein, and carbohydrates and micronutrients like vitamins and minerals. It also uses other components such as water and oxygen.

Macronutrients and your brain

Your brain requires all three macronutrients, carbohydrates, proteins, and fats along with certain vitamins and minerals to do its job efficiently and effectively. However, what your about to learn is that for increased and optimal brain functioning, fats are the brains best friend, not glucose.

- Your brain requires all three macronutrients
- Carbohydrates
- Proteins
- Fats
- Vitamins and minerals

You have probably heard a lot of talk about low blood sugar and poor concentration or that the brain requires glucose. Brain cells, as all cells, must have energy in the form of ATP to fuel the cell. Yes, the body's first choice in metabolism to create ATP is glucose. That being said, though, it is the first choice by default, it is not necessarily the best choice.

Referring to chapter 5, "within the secondary injury, concussions silent partner," immediately following a concussion or traumatic brain injury certain neurological functions may be impaired, making glucose not the best option for sustained brain functioning. Also, during this time an increased amount of particular types of nutrients is necessary to promote healing.

The Secondary Injury

- Glucose metabolic upset
- Not enough glucose production to keep up with the neuron's and brain's required needs
- No fuel or ATP
- More neurons die
- Cells cannot re-polarize
- Increase in symptoms
- Longer recovery time

When discussing macronutrients, it is important to note, that not all carbohydrates, proteins, and fats are created equal. Certain types of these macronutrients should be avoided altogether, like simple carbohydrates, sugars, and processed foods.

Avoid

- Simple carbohydrates
- Sugars
- Processed foods

Proteins

Proteins are very important and necessary for brain tissue repair and brain healing.

Protein

- Brain tissue repair and brain healing
- Organic, grass fed protein options are the healthiest because they do not contain hormones, steroids, and antibiotics that upset the good bacteria in your gut

Organic, grass fed protein options are the healthiest because they do not contain hormones, steroids, and antibiotics that upset the good bacteria in your gut.

Unlike, soy or grain fed livestock, grass fed meat sources contain an increased amount of omega-3's which are anti-inflammatory. Their counterparts, offer meat filled with omega-6's which are inflammatory. Anti-inflammatory options are helpful in reducing inflammation in muscle tissue, including, in the brain.

Grass Fed vs Soy and Corn fed Protein

- Grass fed meat sources contain an increased amount of omega-3's which are anti-inflammatory.
- Their counterparts, offer meat filled with omega-6's which are inflammatory.
- Anti-inflammatory options are helpful in reducing inflammation in muscle tissue, including, in the brain.

Fats

Fats can also be one of the most beneficial macronutrients to the brain, but they too are not all created equal. Healthy fats are Omega-3's, which are found in wild caught salmon walnuts and flaxseed, flaxseed oils, and Omega-3 supplements.

Fats are not Created Equal

- Medical studies show that consuming a diet high in healthy fats like Omega-3's and MCT oil can improve cognitive performance and brain function.
- Healthy fats help in brain performance and also have the potential to reduce the amount of damage to the brain during a concussion due to their ability to reduce the effects of the secondary injury

Medical studies show that consuming a diet high in healthy fats like <u>Omega-3's and MCT oil</u> can improve cognitive performance and brain function. Not only do healthy fats help in brain performance, but new research shows that they might also have the potential to reduce the amount of damage to the brain during a concussion due to their ability to reduce the effects of the secondary injury.

Remember not all fats are healthy. For instance, trans fats and any hydrogenated or partially hydrogenated oils should be avoided.

Hydrogenated or partially hydrogenated oils

- Not all fats are healthy
- Trans fats and any hydrogenated or partially hydrogenated oils should be avoided

- Hydrogenated oils are man-made, and the body doesn't recognize their molecular structure and the body cannot readily metabolize or synthesize them.

Hydrogenated oils are man-made, and the body doesn't recognize their molecular structure as it is not natural. Therefore, the body cannot readily metabolize or synthesize them. Leaving them to build up in your body.

Unhealthy fats also add to inflammation in the body which is the precursor to all disease including but not limited to, heart disease. Before your arteries become clogged, they must first become inflamed and sticky. Then the sludge like cholesterol and plaque builds up, leading to the development of heart disease.

Un-Healthy Fats and Inflammation

- Unhealthy fats add to inflammation in the body which is the precursor to all disease including but not limited to, heart disease.

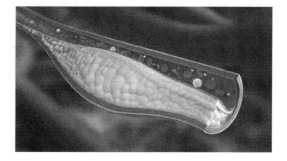

- Before your arteries become clogged, they must first become inflamed and sticky. Then the sludge like cholesterol and plaque builds up, leading to the development of heart disease.

Some examples of Trans fat are lard, shortening found in all prepackaged baked goods, cookies, and most snack bars unless otherwise noted in the ingredients. You can check the labels and look specifically for named trans fats, hydrogenated or partially hydrogenated oils.

Trans Fats and Hydrogenated Oils

For helpful tips on reading food labels and understanding food packaging jargon, you can download our e-Book How to Read Food Labels, https://www.amazon.com/Guide-How-Read-Food-Labels-ebook/dp/B0777H73ZH which will put the buying power back into your hands.

How to read food labels will interpret the jargon and define the tag lines used on food labels by food industries. Speaking their language frees you from being a puppet on a string by marketing connoisseurs.

The information you learn will help you make the healthiest purchases for you and your family.

A Guide on How to Read Food Labels: That Looks Good Kindle Edition

Kindle Price: $2.99
kindleunlimited

What is The Concussion Protocol Meal Plan?

The Concussion Protocol Meal Plan is a nutritional diet focusing on eating specific types of food. This meal plan was designed around the specific needs of the brain for immediate healing during the primary and secondary injuries and through post-concussion syndrome. By following this diet, you will help your body heal from the damage done by the initial or primary injury and prevent the continued damage that can occur during the secondary injury.

This meal plan also focuses on the best way to feed the brain and provide stability through nutrition if post concussions symptoms arise.

The Concussion Protocol Meal Plan

- a nutritional diet focusing on eating specific types of food
- designed around the specific needs of the brain for immediate healing during the primary and secondary injuries and through post-concussion syndrome.
- help your body heal from the damage done by the initial or primary injury and prevent the continued damage that can occur during the secondary injury.
- This meal plan also focuses on the best way to feed the brain and provide stability through nutrition if post concussions symptoms arise.

The Concussion Protocol Meal Plan is based on medical and scientific research regarding how the brain reacts to certain types of food. It focuses on research surrounding the metabolism of glucose and the effect that blood glucose and insulin levels have on the brain.

In specifics, the brain cell's production of ATP (energy for the cell), the repolarization of neurons (aiding sodium-potassium pumps), and neurotransmitter releases and levels (specifically glutamate and GABA).

Based on Medical and Scientific Research

- based on medical and scientific research regarding how the brain reacts to certain types of food
- focuses on research surrounding the metabolism of glucose and the effect that blood glucose and insulin levels have on the brain
- In specifics, the brain cell's production of ATP (energy for the cell), the repolarization of neurons (aiding sodium-potassium pumps), and neurotransmitter releases and levels (specifically glutamate and GABA).

The Concussion Protocol Meal Plan can also be adopted as a preventative diet for people who are at increased risks for possible concussion like athletes, soldiers, and for those battling or genetically predisposed for degenerative brain diseases.

Medical studies show that consuming a diet high in healthy fats like Omega-3's and MCT oil can improve cognitive performance and brain function.

Not only do healthy fats help in brain performance, but new research shows that they might also have the potential to reduce the amount of damage in the brain during a concussion, due to their ability to lessen the effects of the secondary injury.

Eat Healthy Fats

- Consuming a diet high in healthy fats like Omega-3's and MCT oil can improve cognitive performance and brain function.
- Healthy fats help in brain performance
- new research shows that they have the potential to reduce the amount of damage in the brain during a concussion, due to their ability to lessen the effects of the secondary injury

The Concussion Protocol Meal Plan is also equipped to aid the brain through multiple recovery processes like PTSD, depression, anxiety, and other degenerative diseases, because of its ability to impact the amounts of certain neurotransmitters, like glutamate and GABA. For instance, too much glutamate can contribute to seizures and brain cell death while to little GABA can contribute to insomnia, depression, anxiety and ADHD symptoms. Having the appropriate neurotransmitter balance is essential for brain health.

The Concussion Protocol Meal Plan Impacts Neurotransmitters

It is also equipped to aid the brain through multiple recovery processes like PTSD, depression, anxiety, and other degenerative diseases because of its ability to impact the amounts of certain neurotransmitters, like glutamate and GABA.

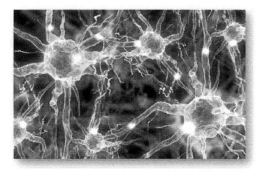

By following this diet, you will help your body heal from the damage done by the initial or primary injury, and lessen the amount of continued damage that can occur during the secondary injury. Chances are you will also obtain a higher level of total body health.

This meal plan also focuses on the best way to feed the brain and provide stability through nutrition if post concussions symptoms arise.

By Following The Concussion Protocol Meal Plan

✓ You will help your body heal from the damage done by the initial or primary injury
✓ Lessen the amount of continued damage that can occur during the secondary injury
✓ Learn the best way to feed the brain and provide stability through nutrition if post concussions symptoms arise

In this section of the chapter, you will be introduced to a modified ketogenic diet concept, what it is, what it does, and how it benefits the body. We will also discuss the benefits a modified ketogenic diet offers when implemented during the post-concussion syndrome recovery phase.

Modified Ketogenic Diet Concept

- What it is
- What it does
- How it benefits the body
- The benefits a modified ketogenic diet offers when implemented during the post-concussion syndrome recovery phase.

You will also learn the formula behind how to implement a modified ketogenic diet, the differences in the Keys2Eating ketogenic diet and others, and the healthiest types of foods to purchase to best assist the body through the entire recovery process.

Ketosis and how The Concussion Protocol Meal Plan affects the brain

Many tests and much research have been done on the effects of concussions and TBIs on the brain and brain functioning. As covered in chapter 5, a multiple of very calculated sequential events happen to contribute to symptoms or an increase in symptoms and can continue for up to 48 hours after the initial primary injury has taken place.

Just a recap, three major events take place affecting brain functioning during the secondary injury.

- ✓ Ionic shifts
- ✓ Metabolic Changes
- ✓ Impaired neurotransmission

An important fact to add, as research has concluded, one major problem after concussions and TBIs is the brain's inability to adequately metabolize glucose for energy. This results in unhealthy increases and drops in glucose levels in the brain.

One major problem after concussions and TBIs

- The brain's inability to adequately metabolize glucose for energy.
- This results in unhealthy increases and drops in glucose levels in the brain.
- Glucose instability affects the brain cells' ability to produce ATP

Glucose instability effects the brain cells' ability to produce ATP. ATP is the energy used for cell function. One of the necessary steps in recovery is the delivery of ATP, the cells fuel, and energy, to keep the sodium-potassium pumps running. The sodium-potassium pumps work overtime trying to repolarize and re-stabilize the cells, to regain homeostasis within the brain. Without a power source to the cells, the sodium-potassium pumps cannot run and restore proper cell function. One of the largest studies of TBI patients to date found that the total averaged monitoring glucose level was a good indicator of whether or not a person would survive a severe TBI or not, supporting a hypothesis that instability in glucose levels have been associated with worse clinical outcomes.

Reduced ATP and energy impacts recovery

- One of the necessary steps in recovery is the delivery of ATP, the cells fuel, and energy, to keep the sodium-potassium pumps running.
- The sodium-potassium pumps work overtime trying to repolarize and re-stabilize the cells, to regain homeostasis.
- Without a power source to the cells, the sodium-potassium pumps cannot run and restore proper cell function.

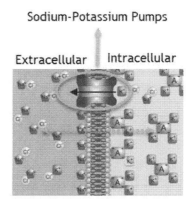

By those studies, regarding the brain's metabolic system, as it relates to glucose stability, one can deduce that eating a diet high in refined sugars or other foods that can cause insulin blood glucose levels to spike and drop is not the best option during recovery. The better option would be to implement a diet full of foods that would assist in stabilizing insulin and blood sugar levels.

The brain's metabolic system, as it relates to glucose stability

- Eating a diet high in refined sugars or other foods that can cause insulin blood glucose levels to spike and drop
- A high sugar and carbohydrate diet is not the best option during recovery
- The better option would be to implement a diet full of foods that would assist in stabilizing insulin and blood sugar levels

It is based on this research and evidence that the concussion protocol meal plan incorporates a different means for the brain cells to obtain energy other than glucose. By offering the brain cells an alternate means in the creation of ATP and energy needed to survive and reach homeostasis, we can avoid the metabolic depression and adverse effects that come with it.

Research shows that by providing the cells with the increase in fuel they demand to recharge and reach homeostasis, you can decrease both recovery time and the amount of damage done by the secondary injury.

All of this adds up to fewer concussion symptoms and decreased recovery time. We will cover, in detail, this alternate form of energy for the cell and how to obtain it in section two, The Concussion Protocol Meal Plan.

This research poses two questions:

1. How do you avoid a glucose metabolic depression and not having enough fuel for the brain cells?
2. Where is this alternate fuel going to come from?

Answer:

While you cannot avoid the glucose metabolic depression that occurs after a concussion or TBI, you can avert the need for glucose by providing an alternate source of fuel.

Since the beginning of time, man has been equipped to survive. The body has an amazing mechanism which kept the human race alive during times of famine. This mechanism is the ability to burn body fat and metabolize fat turning it into fuel.

Natural Mechanics

- Mans survival mechanism
- Kept the human race alive during times of famine
- The ability to burn body fat and metabolize fat turning it into fuel

In normal metabolism, carbohydrates are converted into glucose and used to provide energy for the body.

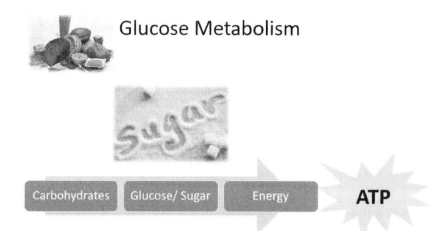

Under some circumstances, like in fasting, or when someone dramatically reduces carbohydrates and sugars, glucose is not available because there is an insufficient amount of carbohydrates to convert into glucose to meet the metabolic and caloric needs for the body.

When this happens, for survival, the liver converts fat into fatty acids and ketone bodies that provide an alternate source of fuel for energy production to the entire body including the brain.

 # Fat Metabolism

- Fat from food is broken down into fatty acids, which can travel in the blood and be captured by hungry cells

- Fat from fat cells is used after fat from food in blood is consumed (this is how you burn fat)

Fat → Fatty Acids & Ketones → Energy → **ATP**

Ketones can be used as an alternate form of energy for the brain rather than glucose. With the implementation of a ketogenic diet, the glucose metabolic issue can be avoided. The brain cells and neurons will no longer be dependent on the glucose for ATP and energy production.

Ketones and the Brain

- Alternate form of energy for the brain rather than glucose
- With a ketogenic diet the glucose metabolic issue can be avoided
- Brain cells and neurons will no longer be dependent on the glucose for ATP and energy production
- Ketones = ATP

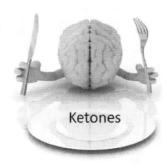
Ketones

Eating a modified ketogenic diet allows the body to reap the benefits of ketone metabolism. This is a viable solution for the glucose depression. Research has also proven that metabolizing ketones for the production of ATP can even be more beneficial to the brain as a source of fuel than glucose all together because of their direct impact on neurotransmitters in the brain.

Ketones VS Glucose

Ketones
- Solution for the glucose depression
- ATP production
- Neurological benefits

Glucose
- Glucose metabolic upset
- Insufficient ATP production
- Unstable insulin and blood sugar regulation

There are a few ways that ketones benefit the brain cells and neurons. Ketones have the ability to reduce oxidative stress, which destroys neurons. Ketones can affect ionic shifts and repolarization or hyperpolarization of neurons. In essence, they can help the cell recharge so that they can achieve their resting potential energy and function as a healthy cell.

Ketones and Brain Health

- Reduce oxidative stress which kills neurons
- Impact ionic shifts and repolarization or hyperpolarization of neurons
- Help the cell recharge and function as a healthy cell

When a cell is not properly polarized or charged it does not operate efficiently and messages are not correctly sent or received throughout the brain, the signals are not clear, and cells can die.

De-polarization in a Cell

Loss of Polarity

- No Charge = No Messaging
- Unclear brain and neuron signaling
- Cells die
- Symptoms increase

The brain must maintain a delicate balance between the neurons and neurotransmitters that help with the transmitting of information between brain cells and throughout the body.

There is a particular neurotransmitter called glutamate which is crucial to maintaining this balance. When there is too much glutamate released the neurons become over-excited. Over-excited neurons do not function properly, eventually, die and can cause many problems within the brain. It's kind of like a bunch of hyper-active children neurons running and screaming around in your brain. A large release of glutamate causes over-excited neurons leading to neuron damage and cell death.

Balance Neurons and Neurotransmitters

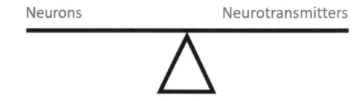

Studies have shown that ketones can block the ability for the uptake and release of glutamate. Glutamate is an excitatory neurotransmitter. An excess release of glutamate or too much glutamate can contribute to seizures and cell death.

Neurotransmitter Glutamate

- Too much is harmful
- Creates excitatory neurons
- Anxiousness
- Insomnia
- Impulsivity
- Neuron damage and cell death

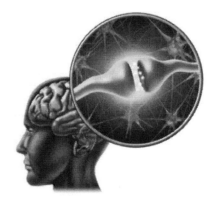

No extra glutamate being released into and around the cells = no over-excited cells. Quiet neuron children ;)

Ketones and Glutamate

Ketones can block the
ability for the uptake and
release of glutamate

Ketones also have the ability to influence another neurotransmitter called gamma-aminobutyric (GABA). GABA is the primary inhibitor of neurotransmission, helping to keep neurons from abnormal firing. For example, preventing glitches in the system. Seizures can also be decreased by the effects on GABA, such as increases its synthesis or production or reducing its metabolism and how much of it is broken down.

The Neurotransmitter Gamma-Aminobutyric (GABA)

- GABA is the primary inhibitor of neurotransmission
- Helps to keep neurons from abnormal firing. For example, preventing glitches in the system. Seizures can also be decreased by the effects on GABA, such as increases its synthesis or production or reducing its metabolism and how much of it is broken down.

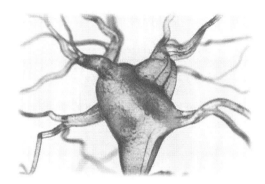

This information is not new to medical science. Doctors first introduced ketogenic diets back in 1921 to treat epileptic children. Since then, though it has predominantly been used in pediatric epilepsy settings, the ketogenic diet has been the topic of study for its neuroprotective abilities.

Ketone Science is Over 100 yrs Old

- Not new to medical science
- Doctors first introduced ketogenic diets back in 1921 to treat epileptic children
- Used in pediatric epilepsy settings
- Been the topic of study for its neuroprotective abilities

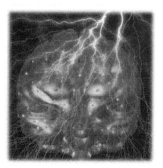

Research suggests that ketones have the potential to protect the central nervous system from degenerative disorders and diseases including Alzheimer's disease (AD),

Parkinson's disease (PD), hypoxia (oxygen loss), glutamate toxicity, ischemia (tissue death), traumatic brain injuries (TBI's), and Concussions.

Ketones have the potential to protect the central nervous system from degenerative disorders and diseases including

- Alzheimer's disease (AD)
- Parkinson's disease (PD)
- Hypoxia (oxygen loss)
- Glutamate toxicity
- Ischemia (tissue death)
- Traumatic brain injuries (TBI's) and Concussions

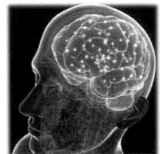

Research suggests that it can do this because of the effect that ketogenic diets and ketones have on metabolism. Many of the degenerative diseases have one thing in common which is the absence of necessary energy for the cells to survive and work properly. The ketogenic diets' ability to uniquely provide the brain cells with the energy they need to survive is believed to be the key contributor to its neuroprotective action.

Studies show that ketones influence the mitochondria and energy in the cell. They stimulate the production of ATP which is what a cell uses as energy. They help the cell create energy in the form of ATP, and in doing so use less oxygen than their counter option, glucose. This means the cells can produce more fuel using less energy.

How Ketones Impact Metabolism

- Ketones influence the mitochondria and energy in the cell
- Stimulate the production of ATP, cell energy
- Help the cell create energy in the form of ATP

Being able to create more fuel while using less energy is also a reason why ketogenic diets can be so useful in providing endurance and can help people avoid the ups and downs of sugar highs and lows.

Ketones and Endurance

- Help the cell create energy in the form of ATP
- Use less oxygen than glucose
- The cells can produce more fuel using less energy

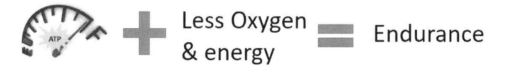

A body running on ketones is like a steady running engine. Many athletes obtain their super human endurance through the use of a modified ketogenic meal plan.

Body Running on Ketones

Ketogenic diets are also so effective in weight loss because in a ketogenic state the body is burning fat for fuel and it reduces blood sugar and insulin levels in the blood. If you are not eating a lot of sugars and carbohydrates, you will not have the need for elevated insulin to transport the sugar or glucose, therefore reducing insulin levels.

Ketogenic Diets and Weight Loss

- Effective in weight loss because in a ketogenic state the body is burning the fat for fuel
- Reduces blood sugar and insulin levels in the blood
- Balances blood sugar and insulin levels
- Hormone stabilization

Studies also show a connection between elevated blood glucose levels, high insulin levels, and obesity, diabetes, Alzheimer's, dementia and other neurological diseases.

Many studies and much research have been done supporting the benefits of a ketogenic diet for improving neurological disorders and helping brain health.

Below are a few case studies for you to read and you can find much more in publicly published medical journals.

Case Studies

- Alzheimer's Disease
- Parkinson's Disease
- Amyotrophic Lateral Sclerosis (ALS)

Case Studies:
A study with 23 elderly with mild cognitive impairment showed that a ketogenic diet improved verbal memory performance after six weeks compared to a standard high carbohydrate diet.

In a double-blind, placebo-controlled study, 152 patients with mild- to moderate Alzheimer's disease were given either a ketogenic agent or a placebo, while maintaining a normal diet. 90 days later, those receiving the drug showed marked cognitive improvement compared to placebo, which was correlated with the level of ketones in the blood.

In a pilot study in 7 patients with Parkinson's disease, five were able to stick to the diet for 28 days and showed marked reduction in their physical symptoms.

In an animal model of Amyotrophic Lateral Sclerosis (ALS), a ketogenic diet also led to delayed motor neuron death and histological and functional improvements. Given all of these very persuasive reasons why a ketogenic diet should be implemented, we will focus on its' ability to reduce more damage to the brain within the secondary injury due to a glucose metabolic depression.

Why didn't my doctor tell me about this?

One reason why you might not have heard about this option as a method for treatment is because medical science does not take kindly to a lot of variables, and prefers a controlled environment for a predictable outcome. After all, once you leave their office, you must be able to follow through with the treatment recommendations. For instance, there is no way for doctors to ensure that the patient will adequately follow a specific meal plan once they leave their office, therefore, not ensuring a set outcome, leaving too many variables on the table. Medical science prefers controlled treatment plans for predictable outcomes. Some argue, this supports why medications work better. Many doctors often voice their struggle of just trying to get their patients to take their medications consistently.

Why didn't my doctor tell me about this?

- Too many variables
- Not a controlled environment for a predictable outcome
- No way for doctors to ensure that the patient will follow a specific meal plan once they leave their office
- Cannot ensure a set outcome
- Medical science prefers controlled treatment plans for predictable outcomes
- Some argue, this supports why medications work better
- Information and education is needed the patient to understand and be able to implement a health plan
- Lack of adequate education and literature for patients

Furthermore, information and education is needed for the patient to understand and be able to implement a health plan. Adequate education and literature must be able to be provided to the patient.

However, with the powerful combination of education and will, this method of treatment can be very effective, and is intended to work synergistically with any medical program.

Talk to Your Doctor About This Program

With the powerful combination of education and will, this method of treatment can be very effective, and is intended to work synergistically with any medical program

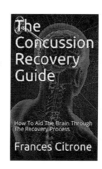

Summary and Recap:

By implementing a ketogenic diet and encouraging the body to create ketone bodies to use as fuel, the brain will not be dependent solely on glucose for fuel and energy production in the cells. The brain cells and neurons will incur less damage due to not enough energy or ATP.

Ketones VS Glucose

Ketones
- Solution for the glucose depression
- ATP production
- Neurological benefits

Glucose
- Glucose metabolic upset
- Insufficient ATP production
- Unstable insulin and blood sugar regulation

The ketone bodies may block the uptake and release of increased amounts of the neurotransmitter glutamate further over-exciting the cells contributing to more cell death and aid in balanced GABA levels reducing the risk of seizures.

Ketones and Glutamate

Ketones can block the ability for the uptake and release of glutamate

All this results in a shorter recovery time. Implementing a modified ketogenic diet and introducing ketones, can help aid the body in its' healing process.

Ketones and Brain Health

- Reduce oxidative stress which kills neurons
- Impact ionic shifts and repolarization or hyperpolarization of neurons
- Help the cell recharge and function as a healthy cell

If your brain is utilizing ketone bodies as energy instead of glucose, the brain can be protected from some of the influxes and effluxes of ions, which depolarize neurons contributing to further cell death. There is also less metabolic disturbances, and ATP production has a better chance of remaining stable. The cells can also keep up with the increased demands in ATP production since there is not the dependency on glucose as fuel.

Ketones and the Brain

- Alternate form of energy for the brain rather than glucose
- With a ketogenic diet the glucose metabolic issue can be avoided
- Brain cells and neurons will no longer be dependent on the glucose for ATP and energy production
- Ketones = ATP

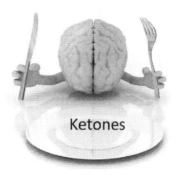

Ketones

It is based on this cutting edge research that Keys2Eating has adopted a modified ketogenic approach when creating, The Complete Concussion Protocol Meal Plan.

The Keys2Eating Complete Concussion Protocol Meal Plan focuses on helping and allowing the body to utilize healthy fats and its' fat storage to provide the brain cells and neurons with the necessary energy and ATP needed for healing and complete recovery.

The Keys2Eating Complete Concussion Protocol Meal Plan

- Conditions the body to utilize healthy fats and fat storage
- Provides the brain cells and neurons with energy and ATP
- Aids the brain in healing and complete recovery

What types of foods to eat?

Below are some healthy and healing food options you can choose from to offer the best chance at a full and quick recovery. We will cover more in detail later in the chapter.

- **Fruits and vegetables**
  Fruits and vegetables are full of vitamins, minerals and other nutrients that are essential for recovery. Flavonoids are responsible for the vivid colors in fruits and vegetables and powerful antioxidants with anti-inflammatory and immune system benefits. Fruits will be eaten in moderation due to their high glucose level. Berries are the best choice.

Slow cooking vegetables on low heat or eating raw ensures the most nutrient dense consumption. Non-starchy vegetables are the best option during the healing phase after a concussion. Leafy greens help the body detox, become more alkaline, and are anti-inflammatory. Avocados are beneficial and are a rich source of healthy fats.

- **Nuts and seeds**
  Nuts and seeds are a perfect blend of protein and healthy fats, packed with omega 3's. Eating regular small snacks throughout the day can boost metabolism and help with recovery.

- **Eggs**
  Eggs are an excellent source of protein. Recent studies suggest that protein in a diet can contribute to promoting concussion recovery. One type of protein in specific can help with brain and muscle tissue repair. Protein powder with branch chain amino acids should be consumed daily to promote healing and brain function.

- **Meats**
  Eat organic, grass fed, unprocessed, meats as a source of omega-3's, amino acids and protein. Wild caught fatty fish is another good source of protein. Sardines can be a quick, easy go to snack with great benefits.

- **Dairy**
  Dairy is acceptable as long as there is no lactose intolerance. Choose organic milk produced by grass-fed cows over regular milk. Grass fed organic butters are an excellent source of healthy fats and omega-3s. Ghee can be used as a replacement for butter as it is dairy free but full of healthy fats. For Paleo or non-dairy followers implement the use of Almond milk (if vanilla, choose unsweetened). Organic no-sugar added yogurt is filled with probiotics beneficial to gut and brain health.

- **Healthy fats and oils**
  Coconut oil is packed with healthy fatty acids and one of the healthier oils available. It is also the healthiest option for cooking and heating. A cooking secret, cook with fats that are solid at room temperature like coconut oil or ghee. Avocado oil, flax-seed oil, extra virgin olive oil, and MCT oil can aid in keeping brain balance and have healthy ketogenic benefits. Those oils are best-used cold pressed or at room temperature. Heating reduces their benefit and makes them harmful to the body.

- **Water! Water! Water!** – You can lose a lot of water when on a ketogenic diet, so drinking water is crucial. Since every body type is different, 8-10 glasses might not be enough. Your goal is to pee clear. Filling your diet with your leafy greens can help to make sure you are getting enough water.

- **Pink Himalayan Salt** – It is suggested to have some sodium intake while you are on a ketogenic diet to help avoid dehydration from losing too much water. The increase in ketones can cause increased urination. Pink Himalayan Salt is filled with key minerals for the body and can be found in most stores. Pink Himalayan salt should replace table salts.

Foods to Eat

- Eggs
- Meats
- Dairy
- Healthy Fats and Oils
- Water, Water, Water!
- Pink Himalayan Salt

Exclude:

Bread Pasta Sugar Milk Corn Beans Rice

Avoid the Following

- **Alcohol**
  Alcohol should be avoided altogether during the concussion recovery process. Alcohol breaks down into sugars which do not promote healing and affects oxygen circulation as well as contributes to cognitive impairment. All this can contribute to further cognitive decline.
- **Processed sugar**
  Sugar by nature is inflammatory. Due to swelling or inflammation after a concussion, an anti-inflammatory diet should be implemented. Stevia or monk fruit can be used in recipes and to sweetened items because they do not raise blood sugar levels and are not poisonous to the brain as other artificial sweeteners.
- **Fried and fast foods**
  Fried foods are filled with oils that tend to be inflammatory. Fast food is never organic and extremely processed which is harder for the body to break down. These types of foods are not nutritionally dense and are filled with toxic effects on the body.
- **Caffeine**
  Excessive caffeine can irritate the central nervous system and negatively impact recovery. Coffee and sugary high caffeine energy drinks should be cut out completely. After recovery organic coffee can be reintroduced. Do not use conventional sugar, instead try stevia and MCT creamers.

Exclude:

Bread   Pasta   Sugar   Milk   Corn   Beans   Rice

- Alchohol
- Processed sugar
- Fried and fast foods
- Caffeine

Chapter 9

Increasing healthy fats and a ketogenic diet

There are two predominate reasons behind the concept of increasing **healthy** fats in a concussion protocol meal plan; they are, to reduce concussion symptoms and to aid in a faster recovery.

By consuming a diet with a specific ratio of healthy fats, proteins, and carbohydrates, you can put your body in the state of ketosis, which just means, your body runs on fat for energy instead of glucose (sugar).

Fat = Ketones = Fuel/ ATP for brain

By consuming a diet with a specific ratio of healthy fats, proteins, and carbohydrates, you can put your body in the state of ketosis, which just means, your body runs on fat for energy instead of glucose (sugar)

The brain is made up of 60% fats. The healthy fat in your brain matter creates *all* the cell membranes in your body. If your diet is loaded with bad fats, your brain can only make low-quality nerve cell membranes that don't function well; however, if your diet provides the essential, good fats, like omega-3's, your brain cells can manufacture higher-quality nerve cell membranes, increasing optimal nerve cell functioning.

Brain is 60% fat

- The fat in your brain matter creates *all* the cell membranes in your body
- If your diet is loaded with bad fats, your brain can only make low-quality nerve cell membranes that don't function well
- If your diet provides the essential, good fats, like omega-3's, your brain cells can manufacture higher-quality nerve cell membranes
- Healthy fats in your diet increases optimal nerve cell functioning

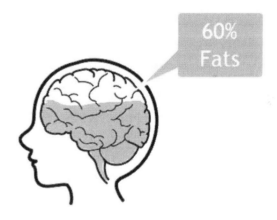

To reduce the adverse effects that certain high-fat diets can bring, the Concussion Protocol Meal Plan implements only particular types of healthy fats that are beneficial to the body.

As I mentioned before, not all carbohydrates, proteins, and fats are created equal. I would not recommend following a ketogenic diet high in unhealthy fats, suggesting to cook bacon and then fry your eggs in the left over grease, or filling up on a lot of lard and hydrogenated oils.

You wouldn't want to rob Peter to pay Paul, or sacrifice your bodies' pH levels, compromise gut health and increase inflammation, just to aid in brain recovery.

Total Body Health

✓ Don't sacrifice your body's pH levels
✓ Protect your gut health
✓ Avoid increased inflammation
✓ Aid in brain recovery

Many of the negative side effects from a ketogenic diet have much to do with the types of foods eaten and the high amounts of unhealthy fats the body is required to consume.

A better option is to remove the unhealthy fats and replace them with healthy beneficial fats, and only incorporate clean forms of protein, specific fresh vegetables, and small amounts of fresh fruit.

High trans-fat diets can lead to increased inflammation which is the precursor to heart disease. However, increasing beneficial fats like heart healthy omega-3 fatty acids are anti-inflammatory and improve blood circulation and help to lower bad cholesterol.

Increasing unhealthy fats can also lead to very acidic body pH level, which in return can contribute to osteoporosis and brittle bones.

Good Fats vs Bad Fats

Good Fats
- Heart healthy omega-3 fatty acids
- Anti-inflammatory
- Improve blood circulation
- Lower bad cholesterol

Bad Fats
- Increased inflammation
- Heart disease
- Acidic body pH level
- Contributes to osteoporosis and brittle bones

What is a modified-ketogenic diet and ketosis?

Typically, when you eat a diet high in carbohydrates, your body converts the carbs to glucose for energy and makes insulin to transport the glucose into your bloodstream. Glucose is considered the "preferred" energy source of the body. This simply means that if glucose is present, the body will use it first for energy.

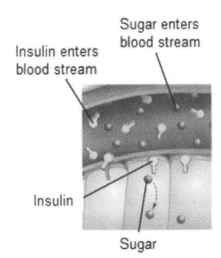

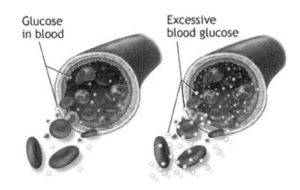

You typically get glucose from your diet by eating carbohydrates like:

- sugar
- bread
- grains
- beans and legumes
- fruit
- starchy vegetables

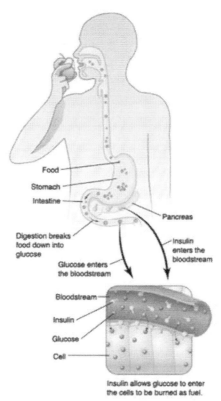

These carbs either turn immediately into glucose in the body or are stored as glycogen in the body to be used as glucose later.

However, sometimes the body will have a low supply of glucose, also known as blood sugar. This could be because a person is eating a low-carb diet.

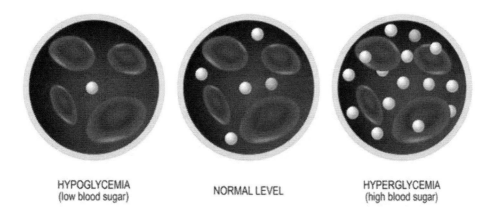

When there is no longer enough glucose for the body to use, it turns to an alternative source of energy: your fat stores. It takes the fat stores, and the liver breaks them down to make energy, when this happens, elements known as ketones are formed.

No Glucose Body Uses Fat and Fat Storage

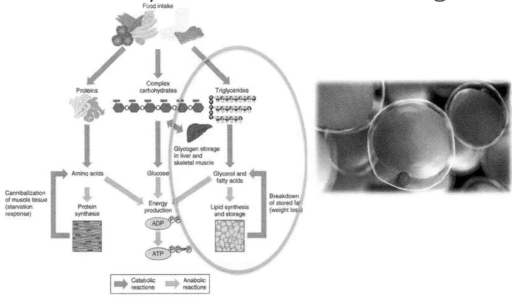

Three main types of ketone bodies are formed in your body when this happens:

- Acetate
- Acetoacetate
- Beta-hydroxybutyrate (BHB)

Once ketones are formed, your body can use them as alternative fuel.

Ketones = ATP   Fuel for Brain

When you lower your carbohydrate intake by implementing a modified ketogenic diet, or high fat, protein, and reduced carbohydrate meal plan, your body does not have an adequate amount of carbs to use for fuel. This sends your body into a state known as ketosis, which is the basis of a ketogenic diet.

Ketosis

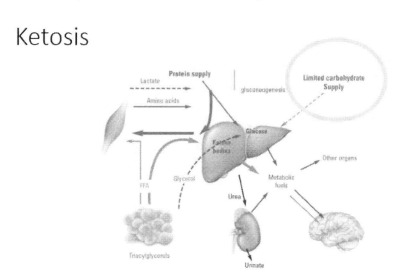

Ketosis happens when the body turns to fat, instead of carbs, for fuel. The liver converts the fatty acids in your body into ketone bodies, or ketones, to be used for energy. As you increase the number of fats in your diet, the body will use fats as the primary power source.

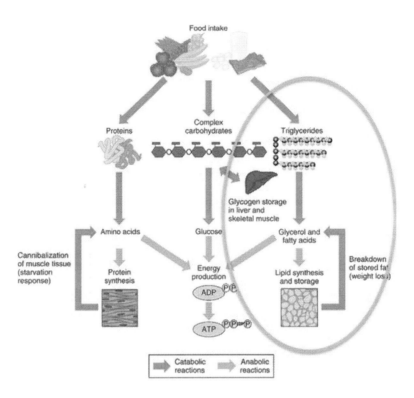

The body has an amazing ability to adapt, and it becomes "keto-adaptive," or more efficient at burning fat.

Keto-Adaptive

- Using fats for fuel
- More efficient at producing ketones
- More energy
- Clarity of mind
- Fat weight loss
- Frequent urination

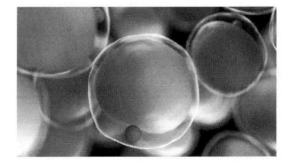

Typically, younger individuals can switch into this keto-adaptive state quicker than the elderly. There are ketone supplements on the market that can help initiate the transition. Before adding any new supplements, discuss them with your physician first. Ketone supplements can be very dangerous for anyone struggling with controlling their diabetes or insulin resistance issues.

WARNING: NEVER take ketone supplements if you have type 1 diabetes because it could lead to ketoacidosis which is deadly.

The process of ketosis is a natural survival function of the body that helps it adapt when there's not much food available. Similarly, the ketogenic diet focuses on "starving" the body of carbohydrates to facilitate ketosis and burn fat while also providing the body with excellent nutrition.

I want to make a clear point. Ketosis is not starving the body, rather reducing carbohydrates and sugars, while implementing healthy beneficial fats in their place. It's kind of like using premium gasoline in your car instead of regular.

Ketosis is not starving yourself

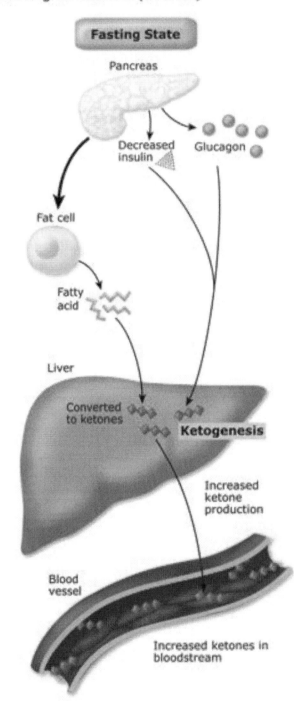

Ketone Production by Liver During Fasting Conditions (Ketosis)

When you are sleeping your body is in ketosis. First, it burns through the glucose storage in your body then it will transition into ketosis.

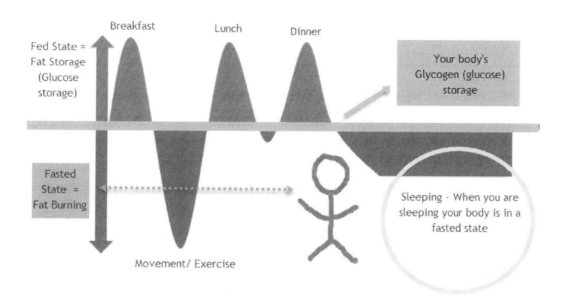

Babies are born in a ketosis state, and breast milk keeps babies in ketosis. Ketosis is very beneficial for brain functioning and development. It is, for this reason, that baby formula options should not have added sugars. Unfortunately, this is usually not the case. Simply, take a look at the first few ingredients of some of the most popular formula brands in stores today. Especially, in a society where childhood obesity, ADHD, and type 2 diabetes is on the rise, you would think we would adhere to nature's intended plan. When we don't, we are doing a disservice to our babies and our future generations.

LOW CARB DIETS VS KETOGENIC DIETS

The keto diet often gets lumped in with any low-carb diet, but some differences should be noted. Not all low-carb diets are ketogenic, and the biggest difference is the level of carbohydrate intake an increase in fats.

For example, a low-carb diet might involve a decrease in carbohydrates but not a large enough one to send the body into ketosis. For instance, the modern version of Atkins often requires that people add in more carbs over time, which may be too many carbs for a modified ketogenic diet.

Also, low carbohydrate diets don't necessarily incorporate an increase in healthy fats. Most individuals usually focus on fat free foods or a decrease in fats to lose weight. This can actually be counterproductive. A dramatic decrease in carbohydrates without enough fats in your diet forces your body to break down healthy lean body muscle into glucose to use as fuel. Since muscle uses more calories than fat to maintain itself you are now burning less calories daily and probably haven't lost little fat if any. This is a common and dangerous mistake that many dieters make. Also fats are necessary in regulating hormones.

Keto vs Low Carbohydrate

Ketogenic Diet
- Reduced Carbohydrate
- Increased fat intake
- Planned macro

Low Carbohydrate Diet
- Reduced Carbohydrate

Ketogenic vs Modified Ketogenic

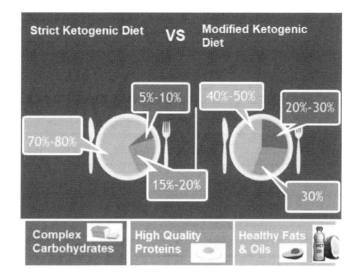

There is a difference between a ketogenic diet and a modified ketogenic diet. A modified ketogenic diet means exactly that, modified.

A modified ketogenic diet isn't as strict as a standard ketogenic diet, and it incorporates a little more wiggle room for increased carbohydrate intake. It conditions the body to be able to switch back and forth between utilizing glucose and ketones for energy.

By following a certain method in eating, you can get the advantages of a modified ketogenic diet without the side effects of strict ketogenic diet.

Modified Ketogenic

- More flexible
- Reduces side effects
- Long term success
- Balanced macros
- More meal planning options

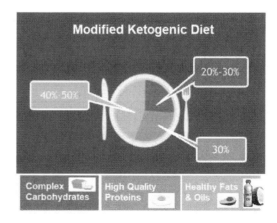

The body goes through a transitional period anytime there is a big change in diet or eating habits. Too much restriction or reduction too soon, will bring on unwanted side effects. Increasing healthy fats can help minimize the side effects of simply decreasing carbohydrates alone.

It is important to follow the design of the meal plan, increasing the healthy fats, and eating enough protein to protect lean body mass and muscle tissue. If you decrease your carbohydrate consumption, reducing your daily calories but do not increase your fat intake your brain will not have the fuel it needs, you will feel agitated and fatigued, and your body will break down healthy lean body muscle.

In the following segments, you will learn how to eat a healthy, balanced, and beneficial modified ketogenic diet.

Follow a Plan

- Macros matter
- Increase brain healthy fats
- Reduce carbohydrates
- Take Minerals and Vitamins

MACRONUTRIENTS ON A MODIFIED KETOGENIC DIET

The general breakdown of a keto diet looks like this:

- high in fat

- moderate in protein
- and low in carb

It's important to note, as you'll see, that the ketogenic diet is not a high-protein diet. As we explained above, the categorization of a diet as ketogenic depends on the amount of protein and carbs eaten each day.

MACRONUTRIENTS ON A MODIFIED KETOGENIC DIET

- High in fat
- Moderate in protein
- Low in carbohydrates

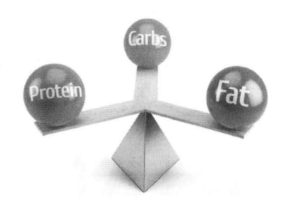

Here are the general percentages of nutrients on a strict ketogenic diet:

- **Calories from Carbs:** 10-30%
- **Calories from Protein:** 15-30%
- **Calories from fat:** 40-70% (sometimes more for certain people)

This is a general range, although numbers can vary if you are incorporating a less strict modified ketogenic diet.

General Estimation

- **Calories from Carbs:** 10-30%
- **Calories from Protein:** 15-30%
- **Calories from fat:** 40-70%

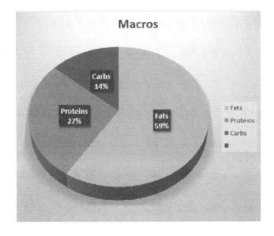

Carbohydrate Intake

A range of 20-100 grams of carbohydrate intake per day will be the average for a modified ketogenic diet.

A range of 20-100 grams of carbohydrate intake per day will be the average for a modified ketogenic diet

Protein Intake

To avoid the breakdown of lean body muscle, you'll want to eat about 1 gram of protein per kilogram of lean body mass

Some factors to take into account when determining your protein needs of the keto diet include:

- ✓ Lean body mass
- ✓ Ideal body weight
- ✓ Gender
- ✓ Height
- ✓ Activity level

To avoid the breakdown of lean body muscle, you'll want to eat about 1 gram of protein per kilogram of lean body mass.

Fat Intake

After you've calculated your carbohydrate and protein requirements, the remaining caloric intake will come from fats in the diet

After you've calculated your carbohydrate and protein requirements, the remaining caloric intake will come from fats in your diet.

Counting of calories are not required on a ketogenic diet (since a diet high in satisfying fat rarely leads to overeating), but you do want to make sure you're keeping general track of your macronutrient percentages versus how much you eat since significant changes in calorie intake can affect those percentages.

Don't forget that the type of fat is important when eating a ketogenic diet. Be cautious about consuming a lot of oils, as they are usually high in omega-6 fatty acids, which are inflammatory in large amounts.

Instead, opt for fat sources that are high in monounsaturated and saturated fats and low in polyunsaturated fats.

The following are some common fat sources on the ketogenic diet:

- MCT oil or coconut oil (as they can be readily converted to ketones)
- Butter (look for sources from cows that were grass-fed)
- Olive oils
- High oleic sunflower and safflower oils
- Full-fat cheese and other dairy products
- Full plant-based fats like avocado

RECOMMENDED FOODS FOR KETOGENIC DIET

- ➢ Meats including beef, chicken and other poultry, pork, lamb, goat, turkey, veal, and fish sources like salmon, sardines, catfish, tuna, trout, etc.

- Fats and oils including nuts and seeds (whole or as butters), oils like olive oil, sesame oil, or high oleic sunflower and safflower oils, ghee, and grass-fed butter.
- Eggs (preferably free-range).
- Dairy products including cheeses, sour cream, yogurt, and heavy creams.
- Low-carb vegetables including spinach, kale, broccoli, Brussels sprouts, asparagus, peppers, and onions.
- ONLY lower-sugar fruits including blueberries, strawberries, raspberries, and avocados (and only in small amounts).
- Herbs and spices as long as they have no added sugars.

FOODS TO ELIMINATE ON KETOGENIC DIET

- Grains including whole grains and breads and pastas made from grains like oats, wheat, barley, rice, rye, and corn. (These items are high on the glycemic index because they are broken down and absorbed quickly by the body and cause blood sugar spikes. Our goal is regulated blood sugar levels.)
- Low-fat diet products that are packaged and processed. (Processed foods are higher in sugar, additives, and preservatives; not good for your body or brain health.)
- Sugar-laden products including fruit juice smoothies, sodas, fruit juices, ice cream, cookies, cakes, and candies. (You can make great tasting berry protein shakes with stevia sweetener as an alternative)
- Unhealthy oils and processed vegetable oils (stick to cooking with coconut oil and avocado oil on your salads)
- Alcohols, because of the high carb content and inflammatory responses. (Kombucha drinks found in most stores, have a light alcohol fermented flavor but are full of probiotics and great for gut and brain health. They come in many flavors and can be used as a replacement for mixes or by themselves as an alcohol stand in.)
- Artificial sweeteners, which can sometimes affect blood sugar levels.
- Condiments that contain added sugar or unhealthy oils.

FOODS TO REDUCE ON KETOGENIC DIET (not necessarily eliminate)

➢ Fruits besides small portions of berries.
➢ Starches including potatoes, sweet potatoes, parsnips, and carrots.
➢ Beans and legumes including kidney beans, chickpeas, black beans, lentils, and green peas (due to their high carbohydrate count) This may be particularly challenging for vegetarians so keep this in to account
**When creating balanced macro meals, some experimentation may be necessary.**

Quick Review about a Ketogenic Meal Plan

- The nutrient intake on a ketogenic or modified ketogenic diet typically works out to about 40-80% of calories from fat, 15-30% from protein, and 5-30% from carbohydrate on a daily basis.

- Although calorie counting is not required, it is important to understand how macronutrient percentages can be affected by caloric intake.

- For example, healthy fats hold a higher caloric % by volume than carbohydrates and tend to keep you fuller longer, but carbohydrates have a greater effect on insulin and raise blood sugar levels.

- Protein and carbohydrates both contain four calories per gram, while fat provides nine calories per gram.

- Not only do healthy fats contribute to brain health, but they can also actually help you burn unwanted fat and stabilize blood sugar levels.

- The key to correctly implement a modified-ketogenic diet plan is to remember that you are exchanging carbohydrate containing foods with a healthy fat intake and a moderate protein consumption. Quality counts!

- Follow your personalized macros plan to ensure you are getting the proper nutrition

- Drink plenty of water to avoid dehydration. When you pee, aim for clear!

Are there dangers to modified-ketosis?

WARNING:

Do not begin a ketogenic diet if you have Type 1 diabetes unless you are taking insulin and are in close contact with your doctor.

If you have type 1 diabetes and do not have an adequate supply of insulin in your body, too many ketones can build up in your blood causing ketoacidosis which can be fatal.

However, under the care of a physician, a ketogenic diet can help stabilize blood glucose levels.

Do not begin a ketogenic diet if you have Type 1 diabetes unless you are taking insulin and are in close contact with your doctor

Ketosis vs. Ketoacidosis

People also often confuse ketosis with diabetic ketoacidosis (or DKA), and it's important to understand they are very different.

DKA occurs when the number of ketones in the blood is extremely high and can turn the blood acidic. Diabetics can get DKA if they don't take enough insulin, become dehydrated from not drinking enough fluids, or become hurt or sick. Other causes may be starvation, alcoholism, or an overactive thyroid.

Symptoms of DKA may include:

- Nausea or vomiting
- Excessive urination or thirst
- Hyperglycemia

- Fruity-smelling breath
- Gasping or breathlessness

Ketoacidosis is a dangerous state that can be deadly if not treated, and it's not the same as nutritional ketosis, which is a safe state achieved through a healthy low-carb diet.

Ketosis is a normal part of metabolism in which your body is using ketones efficiently and safely and only producing a low level of them in the blood.

POSSIBLE SIDE EFFECTS OF KETOGENIC DIET

Some people may experience certain short-term side effects within the first one to two weeks of starting a ketogenic diet.

These are temporary and could include:

- Mental fogginess
- Headaches
- Flu-like symptoms
- Weakness
- Mild irritability or fatigue
- Dizziness

Note that these only occur as your body and brain are adjusting to the sudden removal of carbohydrates from the diet, and they should go away completely once your body has adapted to the low carb intake.

These symptoms can feel similar to a detox, consider that the body is clearing out and adjusting to healthier food choices.

Be sure to drink plenty of water during this time to ease any possible side effects. Increasing Pink Himalayan salt intake can also help minimize symptoms since fewer carbs can cause your body to lose water and this will help you replenish and retain it.

Another option is to lower your carb intake more gradually until you reach ketosis if you feel your body needs a longer adjustment period.

How to Reduce Side Effects?

Help minimize symptoms by drinking electrolytes and by taking a potassium - magnesium supplement.

All three can help reduce symptoms of the "Keto Flu", prevent cramping and alleviate constipation that can be associated with an increased fat intake.

Be sure to drink plenty of water during this time to ease any possible side effects. Add Pink Himalayan Salt to food for balanced water retention since fewer carbs can cause your body to lose water contributing to dehydration and this will help you replenish and retain it.

Another option is to lower your carb intake more gradually if you feel your body needs a longer adjustment period.

How to Reduce Side Effects?

- Drink electrolytes
- Take a potassium - magnesium supplement
- Reduce symptoms of the "Keto Flu", prevent cramping and alleviate constipation that can be associated with ketosis and an increased fat intake
- Drink plenty of water (approx. 1 gal)
- Add Pink Himalayan salt to food for slight water retention (fewer carbs can cause your body to lose water leading to dehydration)
- Lower your carb intake more gradually if you feel your body needs a longer adjustment period

Misconceptions of modified-ketogenic diets and ketogenic diets

There are some misconceptions regarding ketosis. It's important to note that ketosis has been unnecessarily grouped into the same category as starving. But there's a big difference:

During starvation, the body pulls from muscle stores to fuel the body, thus reducing lean muscle mass. Very-low-carb diets, like the original Atkins diet, have been criticized for their extremely low carb intake, less than 20 grams a day, for this reason.

It is dangerous for the body and can wreak havoc on the metabolism if you dramatically reduce carbohydrates and do not get an adequate amount of healthy fats, to supplement the energy demands of the body.

There have also been studies done to answer the question, does a long term ketogenic diet contribute to bone density reduction. In the most recent study done involving adult individuals on a ketogenic diet for 5+ years, no bone density loss was noted. However, there had been previous tests suggesting bone density loss in children. This would be primary to the decrease in the body's pH levels, and the body being more acidic. When the body or the blood becomes too acidic, it draws out minerals in the bones like calcium and magnesium to help balance out the body's pH levels.

One variable is that these previous adolescent studies had the children getting most of their fat from omega-6 sources instead of the healthier anti-inflammatory omega-3 options like found in fish oils. The average American diet consists of highly acidic processed foods and sugars which can also create an acidic pH balance. This is why it is important to focus on healthy alkalizing food choices, and remember, not all fats are created equal.

Supplementing with a high-quality greens powder can help keep the body from becoming too acidic as well as reduce the risk of constipation that can sometimes occur when fiber and grains are omitted. Focusing on alkaline foods choices and supplementing with vitamin D or by taking a good food based multi vitamin can help ensure a proper pH balance.

Someone in ketosis can still receive the necessary nutrition and fiber from lots of green vegetables while staying within a low carbohydrate intake level.

A Modified Ketogenic Diet Including Cyclical Ketosis and Nutrient Dense Alkalizing Foods

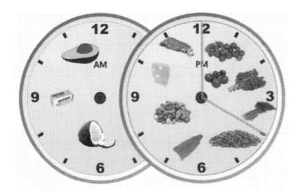

Ketosis is a brilliant function of the body that allowed our ancestors, who didn't have the great access to food we do today, to thrive for prolonged periods of time without glucose. Now, we can still choose to use that mechanism for optimal brain performance, increased fat burning and improved health.

Caution:

Though many of these steps and food options are healthy and can be implemented and added to a seizure management program; it is important to note that this meal plan is not a full ketogenic diet, but rather a modified ketogenic diet and **not suitable for seizure management**. Seizure management ketogenic diets should be followed under guided care of a doctor, in specifics, a neurological specialist. **Uncontrolled seizures and epilepsy can result in death.**

The carbohydrate restriction and macro amounts are very specific for a seizure management plan and should be followed only under a doctor's care. The rule regarding incorporating healthy fats should still be followed within a seizure management plan to reduce the negative effects of high acidity levels, inflammation, and bone density loss.

Chapter 10

The Concussion Protocol

Meal Plan and Recipes

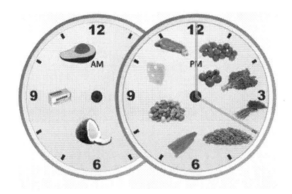

The following meals are specifically chosen to be implemented in a ketogenic or modified ketogenic meal plan. For the best results, follow the ingredients provided.

The recipes created are intended to help the body achieve ketosis, providing an alternative source of energy for the brain to use instead of glucose. Since one of the effects on the brain after a concussion is its' inability to effectively metabolize glucose to use as energy, this menu is designed to encourage the body to convert fat consumed and fat storage into energy.

By incorporating some of the recipes below the body will be able to benefit from a modified ketogenic diet and move in and out of ketosis. This simply means the body will be able to metabolize fat, both consumed and stored fat, for energy.

Glucose Metabolism Upset

Glucose is no longer capable of producing enough ATP or energy for the brain during the necessary healing process.

If sugar or more carbohydrates than specified are introduced, the body will move out of ketosis and begin to metabolize glucose instead of ketones for fuel. Glucose is not the best option for the brain after a concussion, because of the glucose metabolism issues.

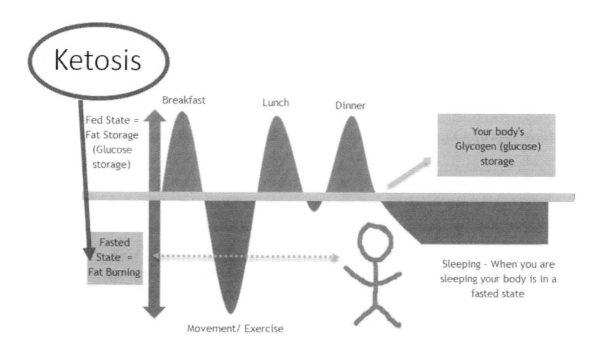

Increased healthy fats and the metabolism of ketones can also help aid in the balance of neurotransmitters in the brain.

The following recipes and foods not only allow the body to utilize the ketosis mechanism or fat burning mode, but it also provides certain nutrients that the brain becomes deficient in due to the metabolic upset that occurs after a concussion or traumatic brain injury.

4 key recipes to eat every day:

Protein and Brain Health Shake

- 1 cup of either kale, spinach, chard or greens mix
- 1 tablespoon of cold pressed Flaxseed oil (found online and in most health food stores)
- 1 tablespoons Barleans Coconut MCT swirl
- One serving of vanilla vegan based protein powder (option Garden of Life)
- 2 cups of unsweetened vanilla almond milk
- 1 cup of water
- Few frozen strawberries (optional)
- 10 almonds
- ¼ of a green apple (green for the pectin benefits)
- Handful of ice (optional)
- Blend on high speed, preferably in a Vitamix or Ninja, until smooth texture

Benefits:

✓ Greens are alkalizing, anti-inflammatory, super nutrient dense full of fiber, protein, and vitamins and minerals

✓ Flaxseed oil helps ward off cancer, decreases inflammation in the body, and is a healthy fat, plus MCT oil to promote the transition into ketosis and provide the brain with quality fats

✓ Use a vegan based protein powder that contains Branch Chain Amino Acids (BCAA) which is specifically critical for brain muscle tissue development

✓ Unsweetened Vanilla Almond Milk has just a hint of vanilla flavor, is low in sugar and carbohydrate in order for the body to stay in ketosis, and is high in vitamin D, while being alkalizing compared to its dairy counterpart which increases acid and inflammation in the body

✓ Almonds add both the healthy fat component and protein

✓ Green apples only, for their pectin benefits

"The Budwig Diet or Mixture"

Cottage cheese/ yogurt flaxseed oil mix — twice a day - eat alone without anything else!

Ingredients:

- 2% Fat Cottage Cheese or yogurt
- Flaxseed oil
- Walnuts
- Organic cranberries (optional)

Instructions:

- Mix 3 tablespoons of flaxseed oil with six tablespoons of cottage cheese/yogurt (maximum 2% fat content). If the fat content of the cottage cheese or yogurt is too high, the flaxseed oil will not mix into it, canceling out the oxygenating benefits of the Budwig mixture.

- Do not stir by hand. Use a blender or a hand held electric mixer for 1 minute at a slow speed. The mixture should have the consistency of whipped cream, with no excess oil.

- Do not add the Walnuts, cranberries or anything else until it has a creamy texture.

- Eat by itself, not with any other foods other than toppings listed above.

The History of the Budwig Diet and Dr. Budwig

- Johanna Budwig, German biochemist and author.
- Budwig was a pharmacist and held doctorate degrees in physics and chemistry.
- Based on her research on fatty acids she developed a diet or meal options that could change the molecular structure and absorption of fats.

Johanna Budwig was born on September 30, 1908, and passed away May 19, 2003, at age 95 due to a fall. She was a German biochemist and author. Budwig was a pharmacist and held doctorate degrees in physics and chemistry. Based on her research on fatty acids she developed a diet or meal options that could change the molecular structure and absorption of fats.

The Budwig Diet or Budwig Protocol is not a "diet," but rather a particular mixture used in many alternative treatments; from type 2 diabetes, autoimmune diseases, heart disease, and cancer to brain diseases such as depression, Alzheimer's, ALS and TBI's.

The Budwig Diet or Budwig Protocol is a mixture

- Type 2 diabetes
- Autoimmune diseases
- Heart disease
- Cancer
- Depression
- Alzheimer's
- ALS
- TBI's.

The Budwig Diet and Cells

Its purpose is to energize the cells by restoring the natural electrical balance or resting energy potential in the cell. Many human diseases are caused by "sick cells" which have lost their normal electrical balance; generally because of lower ATP energy in the cell's mitochondria.

One thing to understand, and this is critical, is that the purpose of the Budwig Diet is to convert oil-soluble omega-3 fatty acids into water-soluble omega-3 fatty acids.

The Budwig Diet and Cells

- Energize the cells
- Restore the natural electrical balance or resting energy potential in the cell

Such a mixture is so beneficial for the brain on any day, but especially after suffering a TBI or concussion. Many neurons and cells are left depolarized needing repolarization. Also, during the initial phase of glucose metabolism upset, such healthy fats help stabilize blood glucose levels and insulin levels, provide necessary

Many human diseases are caused by "sick cells" which have lost their normal electrical balance; generally because of lower ATP energy in the cell's mitochondria.

fats for the body to transfer into usable energy, recharges damaged cell, aids in inflammation, and supports cognitive function.

Benefits after a TBI and MTBI:

- Repolarization of neurons and depolarized cells
- Helps stabalize blood glucose and insulin levels during the initial phase of glucose metabolism upset
- Fats to convert into ketones for usable energy, recharge damaged cell
- Aids in inflammation, and supports cognitive function

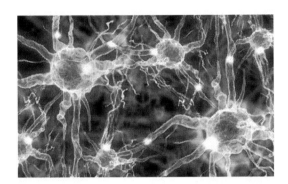

Avocados hold so many benefits to the entire body and are a brain's superfood.

Avocados

Nutrition Facts
Avocados ▾

Amount Per 1 avocado, NS as to Florida or California (201 g) ▾

Calories 322

	% Daily Value*
Total Fat 29 g	44%
Saturated fat 4.3 g	21%
Polyunsaturated fat 3.7 g	
Monounsaturated fat 20 g	
Cholesterol 0 mg	0%
Sodium 14 mg	0%
Potassium 975 mg	27%
Total Carbohydrate 17 g	5%
Dietary fiber 13 g	52%
Sugar 1.3 g	
Protein 4 g 8%	

Vitamin A	5%	Vitamin C	33%
Calcium	2%	Iron	6%
Vitamin D	0%	Vitamin B-6	25%
Vitamin B-12	0%	Magnesium	14%

Benefits:
- ✓ They contain a high amount of healthy fats to encourage the body to reach ketosis.
- ✓ More potassium than a banana and contain magnesium, both help with the muscle cramping that can occur during ketosis and are suggested supplements in accordance with a ketogenic diet
- ✓ They are high in fiber to combat the constipation frequently associated with ketosis
- ✓ Loaded with vitamin-C for a strong immune system
- ✓ Also contain, iron, Vitamin A, Calcium and Vitamin B-6 (pyridoxine) is important for normal brain development and for keeping the nervous system and immune system healthy

A healthy recommendation is to eat at least 1/2 avocado a day, concussion or not.

The great thing about avocados is that their texture can be easily blended or pureed and they take on the flavor of whatever they are mixed with. They can be added to smoothies and used to make puddings because of their rich texture.

When mashed, they can be used as a spread like mayonnaise, or sliced and topped on any meal.

Avocados are an excellent way to get in those extra healthy fat servings, keeping the body in ketosis.

Water! Water! Water!

- Hydration is important
- The brain is composed of 73% water
- Aim for clear

Another important element during this initial phase is hydration.

According to H.H. Mitchell, Journal of Biological Chemistry 158, the brain and heart are composed of 73% water, and the lungs are about 83% water. The skin contains 64% water, muscles and kidneys are 79%, and even the bones are 31% water.

Water is all that's needed. Refrain from fruit juices or other beverages, as they will dramatically increase blood sugar levels and glucose levels in the brain. After injury, the brain's ability to metabolize such sugars is affected, and it can slow the healing process down. Furthermore, sugar is inflammatory by nature and is counterproductive in reducing inflammation and swelling in the brain.

If not enough water is consumed, toxins can build up in the system causing headaches.

The human brain cells contain about 85% of water.

When you urinate, it should be light yellow or clear. The darker the urine, and the stronger the odor, the greater level of dehydration.

Two significant rules on water:

1. When you pee aim for clear, and the toilet. ☺
2. If you wouldn't rinse your toilet with it, don't rinse your body with it.

Chapter 11

Vitamins, Minerals, antioxidants, and Phytonutrients and Your Brain

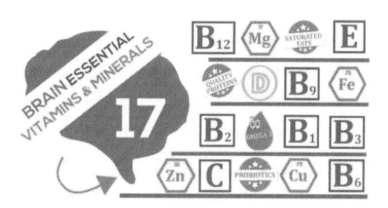

Note: Remember, these are suggestions based on current research and are in no way intended to take the place of the care from your physician. I recommend taking this information with you to the doctor's office to assist in a plan.

The following supplement list is based on specific goals in healing. To reduce swelling and inflammation, heal and restore blood vessels, brain tissue and to regain mental clarity. The reason I am focusing on natural remedies vs. anti-inflammatory drugs is to concentrate on allowing the brain to detox, reduce inflammation without damaging any other organs in the body like the liver, kidneys, and without compromising gut health.

Follow this link to view The Complete Concussion Protocol

https://keys2eating.myshopify.com/products/brain-health-support-kit

The Complete Concussion Protocol Brain Health Vitamins and Minerals

If you have not gotten your Protocol Brain Health Kit yet you can do so here by following this link or going to the address below.

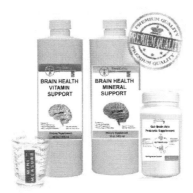

https://keys2eating.myshopify.com/products/brain-health-support-kit

AS THE CONTROL CENTER OF YOUR BODY, BRAIN HEALTH DIRECTLY EFFECTS HOW YOU FEEL INCLUDING YOUR MOODS, MEMORY, ENERGY

LEVELS, SLEEP AND ALL OTHER NEUROLOGICAL FUNCTIONING.

Overall health including brain health is directly connected to your gut health. Recent medical research has proven the importance of nutrition as it relates to the Gut-Brain axis and gut health. As recently featured on NOVA, watch the

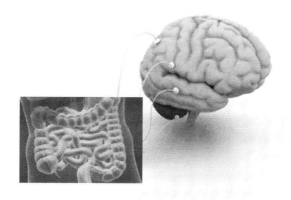

full episode here http://www.pbs.org/wgbh/nova/wonders/#living-in-you medical science is proving that poor gut health could contribute to overall health, including neurological health, insulin resistance, diabetes, Parkinson's disease and Alzheimer's.

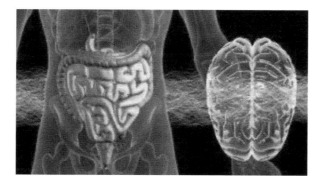

Creating a healthy gut is the foundation of total body health which includes brain health. It is for this reason that our Gut-Brain Axis probiotics are included as part of the protocol. We cover this gut brain axis in detail later in this chapter.

172

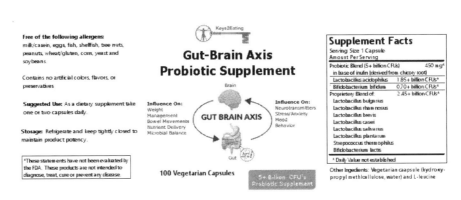

Our Brain Health Vitamins and Minerals are in liquid form to ensure and increase the absorption percentage from a mere 20% in most capsules to a resounding 80+% absorption rate.

PDR: Absorption of Liquids vs. Pills

(Bar chart showing Pills at approximately 20% and Liquids at approximately 90%)

You're not contributing to your health simply by spending money on products that end up in your toilet.

The *Brain Health Support Kit* includes both the **Vitamins (part A) and Minerals (part B) formulas**, as well as Keys2Eatings **Gut-Brain Axis probiotic support**. This complete system supports total body and gut health.

Gut health is the foundation of all health and without a healthy gut biome you do not properly absorb the nutrients in the foods you eat. A healthy gut is also imperative to brain health. Your brain and neurological system are directly affected by the nutrients you take in. This concept is discussed in detail with incredibly interesting data in this specific episode on NOVA, follow this link to watch the full episode if you haven't already.
http://www.pbs.org/wgbh/nova/wonders/#living-in-you

If you are not getting an adequate amount of nutrients, or not properly absorbing the nutrition you eat, your brain health suffers.

When deprived of the necessary nutrients, vitamins and minerals your focus, attention, memory, moods, hormones, and total brain health are compromised.

It is for this reason that we include the Vitamins, Minerals, and Probiotics in the Total Health Support Kit.

The Brain Health Support Kit is a key element in the Keys2Eating Complete Concussion Protocol.

https://keys2eating.myshopify.com/products/brain-health-support-kit

All of our products are **certified organic**, free of binders and fillers and provide effective nutrients for optimal health and weight management.

The Total Brain Health Support formula is just that, a cutting edge dietary support formula with a complete panel of vitamins and minerals for neurological, metabolic and digestive support.

- **Designed to provide an optimal blend of minerals and vitamins.**
- **Less-intense form of vitamin B6, great starting formula for many sensitive individuals.**
- **Ultra-Colloidal suspension for optimal absorption**
- **Separate Vitamins and Minerals, for great potency and flexibility.**
- **Available with or without natural flavoring.**
- **Gluten, casein and allergen-free.**

Brain Health Vitamin Support Formula is a specifically formulated liquid multivitamin designed to provide nutritional support for neurological health. The vitamins and minerals panel can aid the brain in recovery after concussions or TBI's, add assistance in the fight against Alzheimer's and Dementia, help balance neurotransmitters and neurological functioning in children and adults with ADHD, ADD, anxiety, depression and other neurological disorders.

The formula contains a less-active form of vitamin B6, to avoid agitation for those who do better on this form.

This Brain Health Formula provides extra nutritional support for the neurological and metabolic systems, in a very easy-to-absorb liquid form. It has a broad nutrient profile of vitamins, minerals and accessory nutrients created to support metabolic function. The nutrients also support digestion, digestive tract integrity, blood sugar regulation, detoxification, immune function, vascular integrity and circulation, as well as cerebral oxygenation and neurological function.

THE BRAIN HEALTH VITAMIN & MINERAL SET CONTAINS TWO BOTTLES

THE VITAMINS

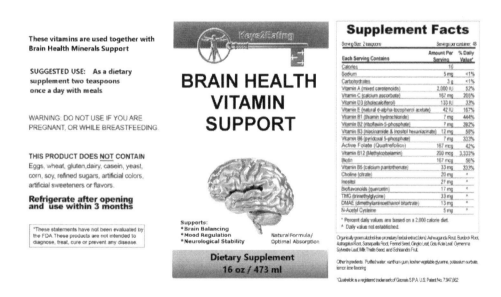

A 16 oz bottle of liquid supplements that, easy to dose liquid suspension. The supplements can be flavored with natural flavor extracts and low-glycemic index vegetable glycerine. They are available in Lemon Lime and unflavored (but still sweetened).

The Vitamins and Minerals are designed to be mixed together and given 1 or 2 times a day, with meals, either in juice or other beverage, or alone with a glass of water afterward.

THE MINERALS

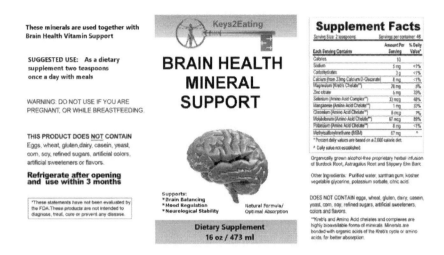

The Minerals used as "Part B" of the Support vitamin formulas are chemically bound to five Krebs cycle intermediaries (fumarate, citrate, malate, succinate and alphaketoglutarate) utilized to enhance cellular energy production. Minerals bound to Krebs intermediaries are far better absorbed, utilized, and tolerated than minerals bound to sulfate, oxide, carbonate, or chloride. Supplementation of copper and iron should be based on individual need, working with a medical practitioner.

ABOUT THE LIQUID SUSPENSION

The nutrients in these supplements are broken down into extremely small particles in a gentle, technologically advanced liquid suspension formula which is readily absorbed in the digestive tract and better utilized throughout the body than conventional powders, capsules, tablets or standard liquid solutions.

Our formulas are distinctive for what is left OUT as well as IN: *We*

- Broken down into extremely small particles
- Gentle, technologically advanced liquid suspension formula
- Readily absorbed in the digestive tract and better utilized throughout the body

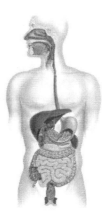

have never used added sugar, artificial colors, flavors, sweeteners, or

sodium benzoate preservative in our supplements and we never will.

Our formulas are distinctive for what is left OUT as well as IN:

We have never used added sugar, artificial colors, flavors, sweeteners, or sodium benzoate preservative in our supplements and we never will.

gluten free & paleo   vegan   soy free   non-GMO   no preservatives or artificial ingredients

What Vitamins and Minerals and Why

B-Complex Vitamins

All of the B vitamins work together synergistically to support critical functions in the brain.   All of the B-complex vitamins are co-factors to each other – that is, they help each other to be absorbed and utilized properly by the body. This is why it is so beneficial to take an appropriate blend of B vitamins instead of just one or two. In studies, B-complex vitamins have been shown to reduce anxiousness and hyperactivity symptoms, as well as, increase serotonin in adults and children.

Animal TBI models have demonstrated that nicotinamide (B3 niacin) yielded beneficial effects including reduced cortical damage, inflammation, and behavioral disruption in animals receiving infusions. It would stand to reason that B12, folate, B2 (riboflavin) and B6 would also be crucial since they are all involved in neurotransmitter synthesis in the brain and controlling inflammation from preventing elevated homocysteine and high nitric oxide levels.

B-Complex Vitamins

• Work synergistically together

• Reduce anxiousness and hyperactivity symptoms

• Increase serotonin in adults and children

• Involved in neurotransmitter synthesis in the brain

• Control inflammation by preventing elevated homocysteine and high nitric oxide levels

Vitamin B6

B6 is necessary for the production and utilization of neurotransmitters which help regulate mood and brain function.   Symptoms of vitamin B6 deficiency include irritability, short attention spans, and short term memory loss. Vitamin B6 also helps with carbohydrate metabolism, which can help reduce carb cravings and crashes.   Shown in studies to improve hyperactivity symptoms.

Vitamin B6

What it does

- Aids in production and utilization of neurotransmitters
- Help regulate mood and brain function
- Used in carbohydrate metabolism, reduce carb cravings and crashes
- Shown in studies to improve hyperactivity symptoms

Deficiency signs

- Irritability
- Short attention spans
- Short term memory loss
- Hyperactivity

Vitamin B3

Vitamin B3 may help lessen the severity of behavioral problems, loss of cognitive function and hyperactivity that commonly accompany ADHD. This vitamin also calms your nervous system so that it may curb restlessness and irritability.   Vitamin B3 helps with delivery of magnesium, vitamin C, zinc and calcium to the brain.

Vitamin B3

What it does

- Lessens the severity of behavioral problems, loss of cognitive function and hyperactivity that commonly accompany ADHD
- Calms your nervous system
- Curbs restlessness and irritability.
- Helps with delivery of magnesium, vitamin C, zinc and calcium to the brain.

Deficiency signs

- Irritability
- Short attention spans
- ADHD Symptoms
- Hyperactivity

Vitamin B12

Vitamin B12 is needed by the body for making and regulating neurotransmitters. Involved in the production and maintenance of the myelin sheath (the protective coating on nerve cells, the "wiring" of the brain), essential fatty acid metabolism and energy production. Vitamin B12 deficiency produces some ADHD-like symptoms such as confusion and memory loss.

Vitamin B12

What it does

- Aids in the production of and regulation of neurotransmitters
- Involved in the production and maintenance of the myelin sheath (the protective coating on nerve cells, the "wiring" of the brain)
- Helps with essential fatty acid metabolism and energy production

Deficiency signs

- ADHD like symptoms
- Confusion
- Memory loss

Vitamins B1 and B2

Vitamin B1 and B2 help deliver glucose to the nervous system and brain. Glucose is the brain's "fuel," and these vitamins contribute to making sure it has a steady supply.

Vitamin B1 &B2

What it does

- Helps deliver glucose to the nervous system and brain
- Contribute to the steady supply of fuel for the brain

Deficiency signs

- Brain fatigue
- Lack of focus and mental energy

Vitamin C

Studies have shown vitamin C to improve cognition and alertness. Vitamin C is heavily concentrated in the brain and crucial to brain function. The earliest sign of vitamin C deficiency is confusion and depression. Vitamin C has also been proven to reduce the oxidative stress that can take place after a concussion and TBI.

Vitamin C

What it does
- Improve cognition and alertness
- Heavily concentrated in the brain and crucial to brain function
- Reduces the oxidative stress that can take place in the brain after a concussion and TBI

Deficiency signs
- Confusion and depression
- Low immune system

Antioxidants

Antioxidants, such as Vitamin A, C, and E, and Bioflavonoids, protect the cells from damage caused by oxidative stress.   Oxidative stress can damage fats, and its primary target is the brain. People under a lot of stress, like our kids with ADHD, have particularly high needs for antioxidants, to help support their body in dealing with the effects of stress.

Antioxidants

What it does

- Vitamin A, C, and E, and Bioflavonoids
- Protect the cells from damage caused by oxidative stress
- Oxidative stress can damage fats, and its primary target is the brain

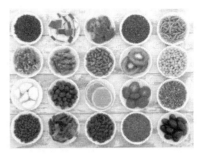

More Information about Minerals and Brain Health

Magnesium

Studies show that 85% of all Americans are deficient in magnesium. Magnesium is very calming and has been called the "anti-stress" mineral. Low magnesium and stress reinforce each other: Stress of any kind lowers magnesium levels, and low magnesium levels increase stress on the body. In studies, people who were deficient in magnesium showed significant reduction in sleeplessness and felt calmer after taking magnesium supplements.

Magnesium is essential for energy production, cell replication and integrity, detoxification, glutathione synthesis, muscular/neurological function, and maintaining body pH balance.

Magnesium deficiency has long been thought to play a significant role in the auditory sensitivity or insensitivity common with adults and children with ADHD. This may occur with a predominance of calcium that can create a magnesium deficiency, facilitating an increased release of glutamate, and resulting in an over-stimulation of the auditory nerve.

One great way to increase magnesium is to add a cup of calming Epsom salts to a warm bath. This is a great way to start slowing down for bedtime at night and help with insomnia. Epsom salts (Magnesium Sulfate) is safe and non-toxic. It can also be added to a basin of water as a foot soak instead of a bath. Following the instructions on the package for dosing and recommended soaking duration.

Magnesium

What it does

- Essential for energy production
- Cell replication and integrity
- Cell detoxification
- Glutathione synthesis
- Muscular and neurological function
- Maintaining body's pH balance

Deficiency signs

- 85% of all Americans are deficient in magnesium
- Auditory sensitivity
- Sleeplessness
- Restless leg syndrome and leg cramps
- Constipation
- Restlessness
- Headaches

More Benefits:

- Very calming and has been called the "anti-stress" mineral
- Encourages bowel movements helps aid in constipation
- Neurological stability
- Relaxed muscles
- pH balance and increased alkalinity

Zinc

Zinc is a major factor in the metabolism of neurotransmitters, prostaglandins, and for maintaining brain structure and function. The expression, "No zinc, no think" is not without merit. Many studies have shown that zinc supplementation is helpful with memory, thinking and I.Q.

What it does

- A major factor in the metabolism of neurotransmitters, prostaglandins (which influence inflammation in the brain), and for maintaining brain structure and function

- Studies have shown that zinc supplementation is helpful with memory, thinking and I.Q.

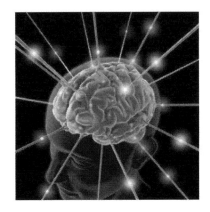

Dopamine is one of the most important factors in the pathophysiology of attention and hyperactivity disorders, and the hormone melatonin has an important role in the regulation of dopamine. Because zinc is necessary for the metabolism of melatonin, it makes sense that zinc is a very important factor in the treatment of attention deficit and focus issues.

- Zinc has an impact on dopamine regulation
- Zinc is necessary for the metabolism of melatonin
- Zinc is a very important factor in the treatment of attention deficit, focus issues and post concussive syndrome

TBI patients have increased urinary zinc losses and acutely reduced serum zinc levels. Human clinical data suggest that supplemental zinc can be used during recovery to improve cognitive and behavioral deficits associated with brain injury.

Zinc and Brain Injuries

- TBI patients have increased urinary zinc losses and acutely reduced serum zinc levels
- Human clinical data suggest that supplemental zinc can be used during recovery to improve cognitive and behavioral deficits associated with brain injury

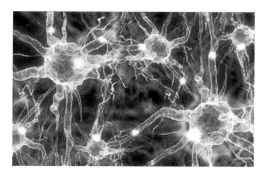

Omega-3's / Flaxseed Oil's / Fish Oils

Important to note: DO NOT take omegas with DHA if there is any bleeding on the brain or hemorrhaging due to its natural blood thinning properties, and always discontinue three days before any surgery.

The same reason they can be so beneficial to heart health can also make them dangerous before surgery. Like aspirin, omegas can help thin the blood and reduce inflammation.

Essential Fatty Acids (EFAs) help with brain and nerve development, cellular communication, oxygenation, metabolism and immune response. During concussion and TBI recovery, Omega-3 EFAs such as DHA and EPA are particularly important for the brain, the immune system, and to help fight inflammation. Many studies show that EFA supplementation can also help with positive mood and attention.

EFAs are considered "essential" because they are needed throughout the human life cycle, cannot be produced in the human body, and therefore must be provided through the diet.

Other studies have shown that pre-injury dietary supplementation with fish oil effectively reduces post-traumatic elevations in protein oxidation resulting in stabilization of multiple molecular mediators of learning, memory, cellular energy homeostasis and mitochondrial calcium homeostasis as well as improving cognitive performance.

Omega-3's / Flaxseed Oil's / Fish Oils

What they do

- Help with brain and nerve development
- Cellular communication
- Oxygenation
- Metabolism
- Immune response

In short, omega-3's help cognitive functioning and brain balancing and are beneficial every day of the week.

DHA supplementation has been shown to significantly reduce the number of swollen, disconnected and injured axons when administered following traumatic brain injury.

Benefits after a TBI or Concussion

- In short, omega-3's help cognitive functioning and brain balancing and are beneficial every day of the week.

- DHA supplementation has been shown to significantly reduce the number of swollen, disconnected and injured axons when administered following traumatic brain injury.

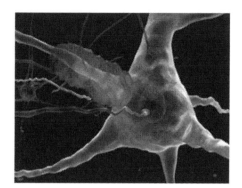

Benefits after a TBI or Concussion

- Reduces post-traumatic elevations in protein oxidation
- Stabilization of multiple molecular mediators of learning and memory
- Cellular energy homeostasis and mitochondrial calcium homeostasis
- Improved cognitive performance

PROBIOTICS

Gut health directly influences brain health and implementing a probiotic can have powerful healing effects on the brain.

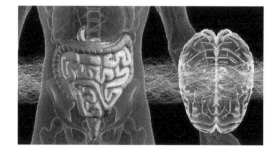

As recently showed on NOVA, researchers have also uncovered connections between intestinal bacteria and anxiety, depression, obsessive-compulsive disorder, ADD, autism, and Alzheimer's disease, among others.

Analysis suggests this link is due to intestinal bacteria's ability to make small molecules, called metabolites, that can reach the brain and impact how it works.

Many people do not exhibit gut symptoms, and if they do, they do not contribute the cause of their symptoms to gut health or lack of gut health. However, many people have an unhealthy ratio of good to bad bacteria living inside their gut due to an increased amount of processed foods, sugars, prescriptions and over the counter medications.

It is necessary to include a good broad-spectrum probiotic to aid in the healing process because of the immediate connection between the gut and the brain through a super highway called "The Gut Brain Axis."

The Gut-Brain Axis

Your gut uses the vagus nerve like a walkie-talkie to tell your brain how you're feeling via electric impulses called "action potentials." Your, gut feelings, are very real.

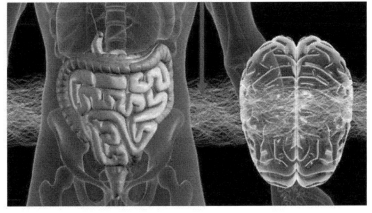

Events that the mind views as stressors causes the brain to send signals to the gut. This is why, when someone is nervous or anxious they can have an upset stomach. If you have an unhealthy gut, a symptom can also be anxiousness causing a cyclical effect.

You are probably aware that what you think about or focus on can stress you out at times. It is also probably no surprise that stress affects the body negatively. However, what you might not know is that your brain health and brain patterns have an impact on your gut health and vice versa.

There is a super-highway like signaling of messaging that happens via the gut-brain axis that influences gut health and brain health keeping them inter-connected.

Changes in a person's mental state, like feeling scared or nervous, can lead to immediate problems in the gut. Do you remember ever having to do a big presentation or take a major test and experience heartburn or upset stomach as a result?

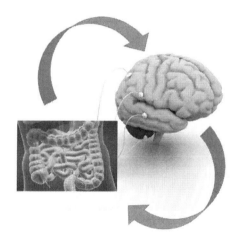

That's the brain and the gut in communication along what it commonly referred to as "the gut brain superhighway."

Events that the mind views as stressors causes the brain to send signals to the gut. That is why when someone is nervous or anxious they can have an upset stomach. If you have an unhealthy gut, a symptom can also be anxiousness causing a cyclical effect.

The following are two key point as it pertains to gut health and mood stability:

> 95% of serotonin production begins in the gut / Healthy Gut = Happy Mood

Gut Health and Moods

1. 95% of serotonin production begins in the gut
2. Healthy Gut = Happy Mood

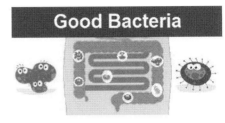

The Vagus nerve is the longest cranial nerve with the widest distribution of any nerve in the body and it connects the intestinal tract with the brain. 90% of all the signals passing along this nerve are traveling from the gut to the brain, not from the brain downward

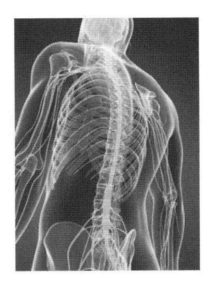

In eastern medicine the gut has been the focus of health for thousands of years. In western medicine, they have begun to make the connection between the food we eat and our overall health.

Gut health directly influences mental clarity and the quality of the neurons in your brain are directly related to nutrition.

Among the many microbial communities colonizing the human body, the gut microbiome is emerging as a major player influencing the health status of the host.

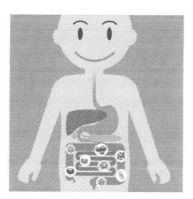 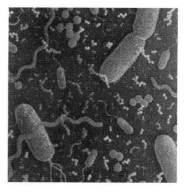

The composition of someone's gut microbiome and "gut health" is established early during gestation period and can undergo a myriad of changes throughout a lifetime.

Medical research has shown that "gut health" both good and bad is inherited from the mother and "gut health" can improve or deteriorate from generation to generation. Furthermore, children who are not born vaginally and bypass the birth canal via C-section or cesarean miss out on vital bacteria intended for initial development of a healthy gut biome; thus putting them at risk for developing poorer gut health.

The complex interaction between host physiology and the gut microbiome is a growing topic of research in neurological health. As noted above and featured on NOVA, the gut biome has a direct impact on brain health and neurological disorders.

Watch the episode here: http://www.pbs.org/wgbh/nova/wonders/#living-in-you

More information on the Keys2Eating Gut-Brain Axis probiotics here

Keys2Eating Gut-Brain Axis Probiotics

- Supports both gut and neurological health
- Influence on neurotransmitters microbial balance nutrient delivery and more

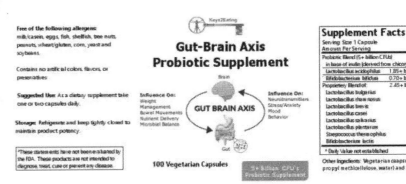

https://keys2eating.myshopify.com/products/probiotics

More Beneficial Items

Arnica

Reduces inflammation and swelling and can be taken immediately following a concussion to reduce swelling and inflammation. Arnica is the first line of defense and can be used without hesitation. It does not contain any blood thinning properties. Feel free to research it yourself and run it by your doctor. Chances are they will not be able to advocate the use of anything homeopathic due to liability and insurance regulations. Many doctors did not receive any education on natural remedies during school.

Pharmaceutical companies are very powerful, and it is big business.

You can find arnica in dissolvable tablets as well as liquid form both can be found in your local health food stores. Arnica is a product that can be kept on hand for sprains and bruising. The tablets should be taken orally for trauma. The gel, oil or cream can be rubbed on sprains, bruises, and swollen muscles to reduce inflammation.

Arnica

Reduces inflammation and swelling and can be taken immediately following a concussion to reduce swelling and inflammation

Branch Chain Amino Acids (BCAA's)

Testing has shown decreased levels of branch chain amino acids in patients suffering from traumatic brain injuries. Changes suggest alteration of BCAA metabolism after TBI may contribute to reduced energy production and neurotransmitter synthesis. This results in lethargy and fatigue after concussions.

Research suggests that increasing protein and in specific taking Branch Chain Amino Acids (BCAA's) can contribute to an increase in recovery after traumatic brain injuries. Dietary consumption of BCAAs restored hippocampal BCAA concentrations to normal, reversed injury-induced shifts in net synaptic efficacy, and led to a reinstatement of cognitive performance after concussive brain injury. The beneficial

BCAA are in the recommended Garden of Life protein powder used in our brain health protein shake recipe.

Branch Chain Amino Acids (BCAA's)

- Restores hippocampal BCAA concentrations to normal
- Reversed injury-induced shifts in net synaptic efficacy
- Aid in cognitive performance after concussive brain injury

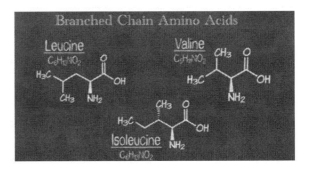

Section 3

"The Aftermath"

A reintegration plan; emotional healing, how to work with educators and employers, and the creation of your personalized concussion protocol plan.

Chapter 12

A step-by-step reintegration plan for returning to regularly scheduled activities

In this chapter, some common questions will be answered, like, when can a student return to school, when can an athlete return to sports, and when can someone return to work?

You will be given a detailed step-by-step reintegration plan for each of these topics.

You will also be provided with a guideline walking you through the stages of healing, in order to make sure you are not prematurely returning to regularly scheduled activities.

By following these guidelines, you will be able to be confident in knowing that the brain has had ample time to rest and heal, and that you are following a complete and safe concussion protocol system.

When to return to school, daycare, or work after a concussion?

By now, you have heard it more than a few times, the first 48 hours are crucial and complete rest for the brain is recommended. After the first 48 hours and under a physician's care, it becomes an individual assessment, as each concussion case is completely different.

There is a saying with doctors regarding concussions. It goes a little something like this, "if you've seen one concussion......., you've seen one concussion. "

Because of the unique nature of every concussion, the best way to fully recover as quickly as possible is to rest as long as symptoms persist.

If you are a caregiver, this means trusting that the other person is legitimate in their symptoms and all of their feelings, even if you think it may be dragging on. Remember each concussion is unique as is each patient and post-concussive syndrome has an agenda of its own. There is no pre-defined duration.

Post-concussion syndrome can come in waves. The best way to make it through, is to ride the waves and listen to the body. When the symptoms go away try something new, if the symptoms return, then stop and rest.

A concussed individual needs to stay home from school, daycare, or work until the doctor says that he/she can return. Most children will need to miss one to two days of school. If your child is school age, talk with your School Nurse or Health Services Coordinator. Adults should take off at least two days of work to access the situation and evaluate symptoms.

Do Not Return Until Doctor OK's

Most doctors will gladly accommodate you with a doctor's excuse. Students may need a request for academic accommodations from a doctor, for the school to make sure all special needs are met during his school day.

By law, an individual educational plan, or IEP, must be acknowledged and all necessary accommodations must be made. Time is of the essence, and a program should be put in place quickly to make sure the student doesn't fall behind or become overwhelmed with work. A possible homebound document can be collected from the school administration office to allow your child to work from home until symptoms lessen and they are able to attend partial days.

School IEP (Individual Education Plan)

When can an athlete or person return to sports after a concussion?

The injured athlete MUST stop all sports and rest until he/she is symptom-free. As covered in *the First 48*, it is important to protect the brain right after a head injury. If an athlete returns prematurely the risk of suffering from another concussion sky rockets. It is during this time that the brain is still recovering from the initial impact and secondary injury. Another hit to the head during this time almost ensures more damage to the neurons and an exacerbation of symptoms.

• Wait for your doctor to say that it is OK to return to sports.

• DO NOT go to practice just to watch. Activity, movement and stimulation does not equate to brain rest.

• When he/she does return to sports, if any symptoms return, he/she must STOP immediately and rest until symptoms are gone for at least 24 hours and the doctor says it is ok.

• A slow return to sports may take several days to several months depending on the duration of concussion and post-concussive syndrome symptoms.

When can an athlete or person return to sports after a concussion?

• Wait for your doctor to say that it is OK to return to sports.

• DO NOT go to practice just to watch. Complete brain rest.

• If any symptoms return, STOP immediately and rest until symptoms are gone for at least 24 hours

• Return to sports may take several days to several months

Stages of Healing

The following guidelines are in congruence with the Mayo clinic and courtesy of Children's Health Care of Atlanta. They follow the neurological guidelines for safe return to activities. Review the stages of healing with your physician during treatment.

IMPORTANT INFORMATION:

Allow 24 hours between each activity stage in the chart. This means that it will take at least seven days to return to full activity. For a patient to move from one stage to the next, he/she must be able to do an activity at 100% without symptoms or problems for 24 hours. If any symptoms return, it means his/her brain is not ready for the next stage. Return to the previous stage for at least 24 hours symptom-free.

Stage 1 – Patient still has many symptoms and problems

• Complete rest in a quiet room.

• Allow as much sleep as possible.

- Limit things that require thinking, focus, reasoning or remembering.

- Remove any electronics and computers from the room.

- Remove any activity planners and "to-do" lists from the room.

- Drink plenty of water

- Eat healthy, frequent meals during the day and at bedtime.

- Increase protein intake focusing on Branch Chain Amino Acids for Brain healing as noted in the concussion protocol diet

- No attending school, work or extracurricular activities.

Athletic Guidelines

- No activity

- Complete cognitive and physical rest

Stage 2 – Patient still has some symptoms and problems

- Stay in quiet rooms.

- Allow as much sleep as possible.

- Allow brief use of TV, video games, texting, social media and email,—less than 2 hours a day. For examples, 20 minutes of brain activity followed by a 2-hour break.

- Do not stress over missed school or work.

- Continue with fluids, small, frequent meals, and a healthy concussion protocol diet.

- May return to school for half days. Work from home or part time.

- Attend core classes only or have shortened class time. Attend relevant meetings then work from home.

- If at school, rest in nurse's office between classes and as needed.

- No tests or quizzes. Limit trivial work.

- Use preprinted class notes. Defer presentations when optional.

- Complete short homework assignments, work 20 minutes at a time with rest breaks in between.

- Talk with school nurse or teacher about academic accommodations from your doctor. Discuss concussion protocol with supervisor or boss.

Athletic Guidelines

- Light aerobic activity

- 10 to 15 minutes of walking or stationary bike

- Light sweat on the brow

- Slight increase in breathing rate

- Walk in park or neighborhood

- Avoid group activities

- Increase heart rate to 30-40% at most

Stage 3 – Patient's symptoms and problems have gone away

- Slowly return to watching TV, playing video games, computer work and texting.

- Allow complete family interaction again.

- Continue with fluids, healthy frequent meals, and Branch Chain Amino Acids protein drinks.

- Patient may return to a full day of class or work.

- Gradual return to classwork, including make-up work, tests or quizzes. Gradual return to normal work day tasks.

- May take one test or quiz a day with extra time as needed, to complete.

- Tell the teacher or school nurse if any symptoms or problems return to notify a parent immediately and allow patient to rest.

Athletic Guidelines – first-week symptom-free

- Moderate aerobic activity

- Light resistance training

- 20 to 30 minutes of jogging or stationary bike

- Arm curls, shoulder raises, leg lifts with weights that can be comfortably lifted

- 1 set of 10 repetitions for each activity

- Supervised play

- Low-risk activities, such as dribbling a ball, playing catch, changing directions, jumping, side-to-side slides, chasing a ball or catching a ball on the run

- Increase heart rate to 40-60% at most

• Add resistance

• Use eyes to track objects

Athletic Guidelines – second-week symptom-free

• Intense aerobic activity

• Moderate resistance training

• Sport-specific exercise

• 40 to 60 minutes of running or stationary bike

• Same resistance exercises with weight for three sets of 10 reps

• Pre-competition warm-up such as passing a soccer ball, throwing a football or doing ladder drills

• Supervised play

• Moderate risk activities, such as balance and agility drills.

• No head contact activities.

• Can sweat and breathe heavy

• Increase heart rate to 60-80% at most

• Increase resistance

• Mimic the sport

Stage 4 – Patient has completely recovered

• Resume all normal home and social interactions.

• Resume all normal school work and activities.

Athletic Guidelines – first week

• Controlled-contact training drills

• 60 to 90 minutes of time on the field, court or mat for specific drills

• Take part in normal practice session

• Contact that is normally part of the sport - only use items that "do not hit back" such as a sled in football

• Recheck for symptoms or problems often

• Free play

• Run and jump, as able

• Full return to physical education (PE)

• Recheck for symptoms or problems often

• Mimic the sport or free play without the risk of head injury

Athletic Guidelines – Stage 2

• Full-contact practice

• After OK from the doctor may take part in normal training activities

• Young patient, with parent or adult supervision, may take part in normal activities

• Build confidence

• Assess skills

Athletic Guidelines – Stage 3

• Return to play

• Normal game play

• Normal playtime and activities

• No restrictions

Chapter 13

How to deal with emotional instability that often occurs after concussions, supportive techniques and how to educate others in surrounding social settings.

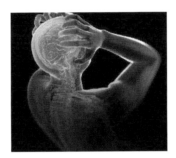

The doctors and neurosurgeons are in charge of protecting the brain through medical procedures, but the individual suffering from the effects of a concussion must manage the aftermath.

Everyone reacts differently, depending in part on the severity of the injury, the quality of their care, and the strength of the social network around them.

Due to the nature of concussion and post-concussion syndrome, much of the battle is an inner struggle with no outside visible wounds and someone suffering can be accused of "milking it" or "making things up." This only further perpetuates the feelings of anxiousness, depression, and other emotional responses. It is so important to have a strong support network during the healing process.

A family guide to emotional and behavioral changes after a brain injury

Each person's injury is unique to their situation. Therefore, each person reacts and recovers in a different way. During recovery, some may experience a few or all of the described symptoms below:

1. Restlessness and agitation - When a person suffers a brain injury they are often unable to focus for large periods of time, therefore becoming restless or agitated. It is important to remember that these responses are normal, and that the person should only be given small amounts of information to process at one time. They will be able to think through and process small bits of information easier than complex ideas.

2. Lack of extreme emotional response - Due to the brain injury, your loved one may not show emotion over things that they may have been very concerned about prior to the injury. This is not because they don't care, but because their emotional responses are simply not there. If the front part of the brain, which controls emotions and behavior, is damaged, it may cause your loved one to act out more. In addition, your loved one may have emotional outbursts or crying for no reason or when it may seem inappropriate. Be willing to give them support and talk to them. Ask them what they are feeling or why they are frustrated. Ask them if there is something you can do for them.

3. Diminished insight - When your loved one is recovering from a brain injury, it is important to know that they may not hold the ability to think clearly or make good decisions. Sometimes they do not even realize that they have limitations. This can be made clear when academic or work related tasks are trying to be completed. Taking the time to rest and waiting to perform mental tasks can help reduce their frustration.

4. Depression and withdrawal – Depression, increased anxiety and other psychological symptoms are not uncommon especially during post-concussion syndrome. During this time try to implement enjoyable activities, get them out for a brief walk if possible and expose them to natural light.

The vitamin D from the sun can help to lift moods and literally brighten their day.

Common Family Reactions

Each family will act in a different way depending on the situation and the people who are involved. The following are a few of the responses that are often seen by those who are affected by the injury, and that the caretaker or other family members may also experience.

- Anger - It is sometimes common for you to be angry with the situation both you and your loved one are in. This anger can stem from the fact that someone you love is now in a situation that does not allow the same enjoyment that they may have had in the past. You may feel that you or your loved one did not "deserve" any of this to happen.

- Questioning - Sometimes you may wonder why this had to happen to someone you love, and if anything positive will ever come out of it. Keep in mind that this is a normal feeling.

- Unrealistic expectations - Family members usually want what's best for their loved one. However, sometimes, this leads to unrealistic expectations of the recovery time and most importantly the loved one. This also adds unnecessary pressure on your loved one. It's okay to set goals, but it is important to set ones that can realistically be reached. Since each person is different, each person's goals will also be different.

- Acceptance -Families who have loved ones with a brain injury are not expected to simply be "okay" with the situation. However, families need to remain hopeful for themselves and their loved one. It is also very important to focus on the progress that has already been made as opposed to all the things that need to be done or changed.

Tips for Success for Family Members and Caretakers

1. Be patient. Your loved one will require more time to put together thoughts and words. Allow them time to answer before you go on to your next thought.

2. You may need to introduce yourself when you come into the room. Sometimes short term memory is affected by the injury and if they don't recognize you right away, it may frighten them.

3. Speak slowly to the person so that their mind has time to form thoughts and reactions to what you said. You do not have to necessarily speak louder, since hearing is usually not affected.

4. Avoid sudden movements of touching or grabbing. These actions should only be used in an emergency or if you or your loved one are in danger. Move slowly and tell them that you are going to touch them.

5. Always treat your loved one as an adult. Although your loved one may seem impatient, or not want to cooperate, it won't help to be condescending and will just make them act out more.

6. Focus on the positive things and not just the negative things. Try to remind your loved one of the progress that they may be making and not how much more they should be able to do.

7. Do not allow too many visitors at one time. Too much activity in the room may cause confusion to your loved one. It may also make it more difficult for them to concentrate on a thought that they are trying to formulate.

8. Be calm around your loved one. He or she can sense when those around are upset and agitated about something, which may in turn cause them to become upset.

9. Do not make unrealistic demands on your loved one. If they feel that they are being pushed to do things that they cannot achieve, it may make them feel worthless and as though they are not making any progress.

10. For those that need hospitalization and have memory loss, bring in some familiar things that your loved one may recognize. Often pictures and stuffed animals may trigger memories that your loved one may have. This will allow other staff to make references to those things when family members are not around.

11. Join a support group. Knowing that there are others in your situation may help you to cope with your situation. Visit with and talk with your pastor or church leaders, and confide in those around you. Share with them your frustrations as well the good things that are being accomplished.

You can connect with others that have been affected by concussions or TBI's by simply joining our Facebook community if you have not already. https://www.facebook.com/Keys2Concussions/

Chapter 14

How to work with educators and employers: laws and regulations.

School and work related programs and laws will vary depending upon the country, providence an even state that you live in. For those living outside of the United States, you will have to research what programs are available for you in your area. For those living in the United States, laws vary from state to state, however, there is a general federal standard for programs.

The education laws are enforced and part of legislation within a public school system, but private schools also have to offer educational solutions for their students with special medical needs. Private school options might vary and might not necessarily be free because they are not funded by the state, and might include a private tutor.

School and educational homebound instructions are much different than homeschooling program. Homebound instruction is provided by the state through the public school system

at no charge to the family, including all materials and instruction (not in a private school system), whereas, home schooling instruction is given by a parent or guardian using the materials of his/her choice.

Homebound vs Homeschooling Programs

School Homebound Programs
- provided by the state through the public school system
- no charge to the family
- includes all materials and instruction
- not always available in a private school system (private schools are not made to follow all public education regulation)
- only sick children are on homebound instruction

Homeschooling Programs
- homeschooling instruction is given by a parent or guardian using the materials of his/her choice
- any student can be homeschooled

Most children who receive homebound services only receive them temporarily due to an illness, surgery, or accident. Most of the programs are designed for these types of situations and timing to allow the student full recovery time while preventing them from falling too far behind.

Due to the nature of a concussion or TBI, and the brain is the injury, it is important not to prematurely begin instruction until initial symptoms have stopped.

Complete brain rest is imperative during the first phase of healing which occurs immediately following the head injury.

After the initial head injury symptoms have passed a student can return to school. If post-concussion symptoms persist partial attendance may be necessary contingent upon how the student is feeling on a day to day basis.

This part of the recovery can be a tedious and be a lonely road for the concussed as the injuries are not apparent from the outside. Though it is important to encourage a return to regular scheduled activities and life a certain amount of validity of the struggle can be helpful in the healing process.

Post-concussion or post-concussive symptoms can make it difficult to complete tasks and academic lessons or work and should be done in short durations with complete rest in between. Refer back to chapter 9, for the re-integration stages for a safe return to regularly scheduled activities.

Over exhausting and pushing the individual recovering will not help them to meet the academic objectives or goals. It can actually do the exact opposite, resulting in not only brain fatigue and symptom exacerbation but also emotional stress and increased post-concussion symptoms including depression. Patience and encouragement is key during this time.

Legal Requirements for Homebound Instructions

Each state is allowed to develop its own guidelines for homebound instruction and even school districts within the state may vary in specific guidelines. There is not federal guidance governing homebound instruction within education laws, however, like any placement homebound instruction must be individualized to fulfill the student's Individualized Education Plan (IEP).

Legal Requirements for Homebound Instructions

- Each state is allowed to develop its own guidelines
- School districts within the state may vary in specific guidelines
- No federal guidance governing homebound instruction within education laws, however
- Any placement homebound instruction <u>must</u> be individualized to fulfill the student's Individualized Education Plan (IEP) <u>(this is your loop hole to guarantee your students needs are met and enough hours of tutoring are given</u>

The individual state guidelines vary dramatically both in how the homebound instruction is offered, and also in how much instruction is required. For instance, in many states a student is not eligible and cannot apply for homebound instruction until they miss a consecutive 10-20 days of school.

While in other states, homebound education must be started within 10 days once prescribed by a physician. Some states only require two one hour sessions per week. This means only two hours with an instructor, so that little time should be well planned out utilizing it on items that the student needs help with not necessarily busy work they can do with the help of a parent or guardian.

Other states require 2 hours per course taken in the student's schedule. This is much more adequate and gives more time for tutorial instruction.

As previously mentioned, in addition to state requirements, each district may have its own policies. For example, some districts may provide homebound instruction during school hours, while others may provide it after school hours.

Based on the current federal legislation the following homebound instruction standards can be defined:

- Schools are not required to offer any particular amount of homebound instruction. The instruction amount must be sufficient in duration to meet the goals of the IEP (Individualized Education Plan). There are no minimums or maximums.
- Schools are required to offer related services to children receiving homebound services, provided by direct providers (such as physical therapists or augmentative communication specialists), in order to meet the requirements of the child's IEP.
- A parent, guardian, or family-provided nurse/care attendant must be present during the sessions.
- Services are almost always provided at home or at a hospital/inpatient facility.
- The homebound instruction must fulfill the child's IEP.
- A physician's referral for homebound education is almost universally required.
- Children requiring special education services in the IEP must receive services from a special education teacher.

How to Overcome Obstacles Presented by Homebound Instruction

Two hurdles in homebound education, outside the obvious challenges during recovery, are the small number of hours of tutorial instruction and lack of related services to assist in the immediate needs of the student while they are recovering.

Two hurdles in homebound education

- The small number of hours of tutorial instruction
- Lack of related services to assist in the immediate needs of the student while they are recovering

I personally came across this issue during my son's first concussion. Without this knowledge explaining how to overcome the obstacle of not enough instructional time and the waiting game, we spent hundreds of our own dollars on private tutors unnecessarily. If I had the simple approach I am about to tell you, I believe my son would not have fallen so far behind and would have had much less stress place on him.

A key way to address your student's need for more instruction hours is to refer to their "Individualized Education Plan". These words hold power and leverage, and are recognized at both the state and federal level.

When you discuss a plan with your student's school, remember the school district MUST provide however many hours are required to meet the students individualized education plan (IEP) goals. You need to specifically use those words and refer to federal regulations. You are not being pushy or rude, however, you are and advocate for your student. If you don't fight for them, who will?

Individualized Education Plan

These words hold power and leverage, and are recognized at both the state and federal level

IEP Template for Present Levels of Performance

1. Evaluation results
2. Present levels of performance for each need area:
   - Current functioning
   - Strengths of the student
   - Needs of the student
3. Effect of student's needs on his/her involvement and progress in the general curriculum (or appropriate activities for preschool students)
4. Student needs relating to special factors (special consideration)

School districts also need to provide technology services and the necessary technology to keep at home in order for the student to meet their IEP goals. Related services to meet their IEP goals include direct therapies required to access the curriculum at home.

Another common stumbling block in a homebound program is the criteria of certain periods of days absent before the student is eligible for the homebound program services to begin, and that it must be consistent and not intermittent. I found this rule to be very stringent during the recovery process, due to the fact that some days are better than others. You want to encourage your student to attend classes without losing the option of returning home if they are either not yet ready or symptoms return.

Create an open door policy by providing a physician's note detailing the specifics of the recovery plan including the option to return home if symptoms return.

Homebound solution

- Create an open door policy by providing a physician's note detailing the specifics of the recovery plan including the option to return home if symptoms return

In order to overcome such restrictions, the provision of intermittent homebound services should be included in the IEP. For example, a student who misses school frequently due to migraines, vertigo or other concussion or post-concussive syndrome symptoms should have a plan in the IEP that would allow an instructor to come to the home whenever the child misses more than one day of school.

How to Maximize Homebound Instruction

Constant communication between the school, homebound instructor, and family is crucial in ensuring your student receives the best instruction and care needed to keep them caught up in school, as well as, keeping them emotionally calm and focused on complete recovery.

If your student is well enough to return to school they should be encouraged to do so. Sometimes they may need a little encouraging nudge to return to their daily routine. Students should have the option to return to school on a partial schedule, giving them freedom to gradually re-integrate back into their schedule. Younger children especially may find it harder to give up the extra TLC they are receiving back home, but it is in their best interest to get back to a healthy routine. Initially attending school for partial days may help make their return easier.

Constant communication between the school, homebound instructor, and family

- Ensuring your student receives the best instruction
- Individual Education Plan (IEP) created and followed
- Personal care given keeping them emotionally calm and focused on complete recovery

Finally, homebound instruction does not have to be isolating. Students who cannot attend school should still be encouraged to participate in classroom activities or groups. One way to make that possible is via Skype and email.

Accommodations in the workplace

When it comes to government legislation, there are separate laws dependent upon whether or not the injury took place at work or at home. The employer must provide more accommodations if it was a work related accident vs something that happened away from work on the employees own time. If an employee receives a concussion at work they are eligible to file a workman's comp insurance claim. The laws may vary depending upon the size of the business and the state in which the business is registered.

Non Workman's Comp Claims

Unlike in the educational system, there are not federal or state regulations set in place for every business regarding absences due to accidents such as concussions or TBI's. This is not necessarily a bad thing, because more government regulation in the business sector is not the answer. It will be up to your employer or supervisor to work out a temporary leave of absence.

However, there are some laws that help an employee keep their job and make arrangements until they recover and can return to work, but they do not mandate a paid leave. Contrary to popular belief, there is no general legal requirement that employers give employees sick leave. While most employers do in fact give employees some paid time off each year to be used for sick leave, the law does not require employers to do so in most circumstances.

Under some circumstances, however, the law does require employers to permit employees to take unpaid time off from work for illness, without negative consequences for the employees. Leave from work may be required by the Family and Medical Leave Act or to accommodate a disability.

For more information on these existing requirements google your states, state and local paid sick leave laws.

According to the department of labor, though there are no federal legal requirements for paid sick leave, certain companies are subject to the Family and Medical Leave Act (FMLA), the Act does require unpaid sick leave. FMLA provides for up to 12 weeks of unpaid leave for certain medical situations for either the employee or a member of the employee's immediate family. In many instances paid leave may be substituted for unpaid FMLA leave. If agreed to by the employer, or if the employee has paid sick days available in their contract.

The criteria for the FMLA is as follows, employees are eligible to take FMLA leave if they have worked for their employer for at least 12 months, and have worked for at least 1,250 hours over the previous 12 months, and work at a location where at least 50 employees are employed by the employer within 75 miles.

If available, the human resource department would be a good place to start for information. An important rule of thumb, is to keep lines of communication open with supervisor or employer, and provide the proper medical excuses describing the reasons and estimated duration of the absence.

Workman's Comp Claims

An employee who suffers a head injury is eligible for workers' compensation benefits. Those benefits include reimbursement for medical and therapy bills, out-of-pocket expenses (medications, bandages, hospital parking fees, etc.), and approximately two-thirds of lost wages. Specifics of compensation will vary depending upon the size of the company and the state in which it is registered.

Not all employers are required to carry workers' comp insurance. Depending on the state, some smaller companies with a limited number of employees are exempt from having to provide coverage. Other employers may be exempt from state requirements because they have enough assets to provide intra-company insurance with benefits equal to, or better than those provided under the state's workers' compensation laws. These companies are referred to as self-certified.

Following a workplace injury, you must file a "first report of injury" form (DWC-1) with your employer as soon as possible. This is a worker's compensation form that may differ between states. You can google your states specific DWC-1 form and download it online instead of waiting on your employer to provide you with one. There are multiple DWC forms to submit to keep record of the medical costs throughout the term of care and to help specify the benefits the employee is qualified to receive.

"First Report of Injury" form (DWC-1)

- Following a workplace injury, you MUST file a "first report of injury" form (DWC-1) with your employer ASAP

- A form that may differ between states

- You can google your states specific DWC-1 form and download it online instead of waiting on your employer to provide you with one

- There are multiple DWC forms to submit to keep record of the medical costs throughout the term of care and to help specify the benefits the employee is qualified to receive

- After completing the form, your employer should provide you with a list of approved physicians, and you'll choose one as your primary treating physician. These physicians are paid by the workers' comp insurance company

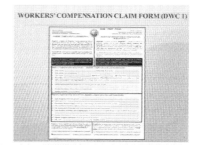

After completing the form, your employer should provide you with a list of approved physicians, and you'll choose one as your primary treating physician. These physicians are paid by the workers' comp insurance company. With a head injury it is important to be evaluated immediately due to nature of the injury and the fact that head injuries, even ones that look harmless, could be life threatening if swelling occurs in the right place.

In the case of an emergency visit, it is important to let the examining hospital or physician know that it was a work related accident. Most office visits and ER paperwork will ask the question whether or not the injury was obtained at work.

The workers' comp physician makes an initial evaluation of your head injury, and because you sustained a blow to the head, there's a chance you could be referred to a neurologist or neurosurgeon for treatment and follow-up. If a head trauma specialist isn't on the approved list, you should be allowed to see a private specialist of your own choosing.

DON'T WAIT TO SEE A DOCTOR

- With a head injury it is important to be evaluated immediately due to nature of the injury
- Even ones that look harmless, could be life threatening if swelling occurs in the right place
- In the case of an emergency visit, it is important to let the examining hospital or physician know that it was a work related accident
- Most office visits and ER paperwork will ask the question whether or not the injury was obtained at work

Workers' compensation, also called workman's compensation or workers' comp, is a type of insurance that pays benefits if you're injured on the job. Workers' comp insurance may pay a portion of your wages and all approved medical expenses directly related to your injury. It may also cover vocational rehabilitation, temporary and extended pay in the circumstance of long-term disability, and even death benefits.

Workers' Compensation/ Workman's Comp

- A type of insurance that pays benefits if you're injured on the job
- Workman's comp insurance may pay a portion of your wages and all approved medical expenses directly related to your injury
- It may also cover vocational rehabilitation, temporary and extended pay in the circumstance of long-term disability, and even death benefits.

What Workers' Compensation Insurance Covers

Lost Wages

When figuring out lost wages, two items are considered and calculated. The injured employees previous years' salary and the percentage in which the doctor has ruled

him/her unable to work. In most states, workers' comp insurance coverage pays an injured worker approximately 66 percent (two-thirds) of his normal weekly wages.

The formula used to determine the exact amount of partial wage payments varies from state to state. The amount of weekly benefits for total disability is usually 60% or 2/3 (66 2/3%) of the employee's pre-injury average weekly wage (AWW). AWW is the employee's actual earnings, including overtime, for a certain number of weeks before the injury (up to 52), divided by that number of weeks.

Lost Wages Formula

- The formula used to determine the exact amount of partial wage payments varies from state to state
- The amount of weekly benefits for total disability is usually 60% or 2/3 (.66 or 2/3%) of the employee's pre-injury average weekly wage (AWW)
- AWW is the employee's actual earnings, including overtime, for a certain number of weeks before the injury (up to 52), divided by that number of weeks.

$$\$ \text{Paid} = .66 * \text{Average Weekly Wage (AWW)}$$

The following is an example of this formula for partial wage reimbursement.

In the state of New York, a worker who becomes totally or partially disabled is unable to return to work for more than seven days receives payment for lost wages based on his weekly pay for the previous year.

The formula for calculating the allowable amount of lost wages [AAW] in New York uses 2/3 of the last year's weekly pay, multiplied by the % of current disability.

If the injured worker's weekly pay for last year was $600.00 and the doctors certify him as 100% disabled, the formula for the money he would receive would be:

$600.00 x 2/3 = $400.00 x 100% disability = $400.00 per week in lost wages

If the doctor only certified him as 50% disabled, the formula would be:

$600.00 x 2/3 = $400.00 x 50% disability = $200.00 per week in lost wages

The length of time for receiving these partial wage payments is determined by the type of injury and extent of medical treatment required. In addition, the duration is set by each state's maximum pay-out period regulations.

For example, an injured worker in New Mexico can receive wage compensation for up to 700 weeks, depending on the percentage and type of disability. In California, an injured worker can receive wage compensation for up to 204 weeks, also depending on the nature of the injury.

Approved Medical Expenses

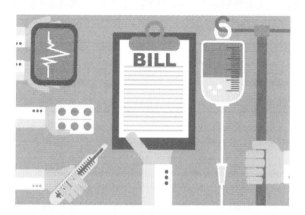

In most cases, workers' compensation benefits include payment for medical and therapeutic expenses.

Medical expenses normally include hospital costs and required diagnostic tests, such as MRIs and CT scans. Related out-of-pocket expenses, such as wheelchairs, crutches and, in some cases, transportation to and from treatment centers, can be covered. More liberal coverage may include counseling, pain therapy, holistic remedies, and acupuncture. In most cases, experimental treatment is not covered.

Remember, if you're injured on the job, generally you must ask your employer for a list of doctors approved by his workers' comp insurance company. If you choose to see a doctor that is not part of the employer's workman comp insurance plan your medical bills for that doctor may not be covered. Furthermore, each state has its own time period within which you must choose a doctor and be evaluated. Time periods may range from 30 to 90 days. If you don't get a medical evaluation within the required time period, you may lose your right to continue your claim.

After you've been evaluated by an employer-approved doctor, you may seek an independent opinion from a doctor of your own choosing. You may have to pay the costs out of your own pocket, although in some states you can be reimbursed before your claim is completed. Be sure to request copies of your diagnosis, prognosis and any other notes relevant to your injury from your own doctor(s). You must submit that information to the workers' comp insurance company.

Physical and Vocational Rehabilitation

Most states' workers' comp laws provide injured employees the right to physical and vocational rehabilitation.

Physical rehabilitation covers medical and therapeutic care. This includes physical therapy to assist in coping with the effects of your injury and to help you return to your job duties. Physical therapy frequently covers the cost of licensed physical therapists, massage therapists, and others certified to assist with the healing process.

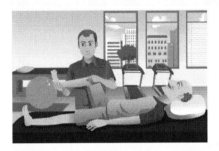

Vocational rehabilitation provides various tools to prepare you for a new job with your current employer or when seeking a job elsewhere. Vocational rehabilitation coverage varies from state to state and may include:

- Retraining for a different type of job within the company
- Education and tuition payments for retraining
- Résumé and employment application assistance
- Assistance in searching for a new job with another company
- Specialized testing to determine if you have skills for a new career
- Counseling regarding employment expectations and qualifications

Type of Disability and Benefit Duration

The duration of your workers' comp coverage normally depends on the type of injury or disability you sustained. There are four types of disability categories used in calculating the amount and duration of your benefits:

1. *Temporary Total Disability* is the most common type. This is an on-the-job injury that completely prevents you from working for a limited amount of

time. Benefits normally end when you're medically cleared to return to work.

2. *Temporary Partial Disability* prevents you from doing some, but not all, of your job duties for a limited amount of time. Benefits normally end when you're medically cleared to resume all of your former job duties.

3. *Permanent Total Disability* prevents you from ever returning to work, whether for your current employer or another employer. If the injury results in death, benefits will be paid to immediate family members for as long as state law permits. If death does not occur, you have the option of retraining for a new and different type of work. Your disability benefits cease when you begin a new job.

4. *Permanent Partial Disability* is permanent injury that partially impairs your ability to work. This type of disability is often controversial. Injured employees often disagree with the medical determination that their ability to work is only partially impaired when they're considered permanently disabled.

The Compensation Bargain - Pros and Cons

Compensation bargain is an informal term relating to workers' comp coverage. It alludes to the trade-offs employers and employees must make under the workers' compensation system.

Workers' comp insurance is a form of no-fault insurance for on-the-job injuries. It serves employers because their employees are not permitted to sue them for negligence. This exempts employers from having to pay for an injured employee's pain and suffering. Payments are limited to partial wage reimbursement and medical/therapeutic benefits (and death benefits where applicable).

It serves employees because they don't have to fight with an insurance company or file a lawsuit to prove their employer was negligent. If an employee is injured on the job, she receives partial wage reimbursement and medical/therapeutic coverage without having to file a lawsuit.

One of the main disadvantages for employees is the partial wages and medical/therapeutic costs. This can be especially frustrating when an employee is dependent on a full paycheck to support a family.

Federal and state laws and regulation are subject to change. Contact your state for the most current rulings regarding your personal situation and review specific guidelines if you feel like your rights are being overlooked.

Chapter 15

A Personalized Action Plan

Creating a Concussion Plan and a Concussion Recovery Kit

Research has proven that the best way to learn something and ensure change is through implementation.

You haven't truly learned something until you can apply the knowledge and implement it into your own life.

This is why this chapter is one of the most important chapters in the book.

Up to this point, you have learned how to define and recognize a concussion, the domino effect and metabolic cascade that takes place in the brain after a concussion occurs, and an entire concept of eating for optimal brain health, better nutrition, and total health.

What you have learned

- How to define and recognize a concussion
- The domino effect and metabolic cascade that takes place in the brain after a concussion occurs
- An entire concept of eating for brain health, better nutrition, and total health

WOW!!!!

<u>So now what?</u>

It is time to construct your path towards complete integration, water those seeds of knowledge, put some roots on this new found plan and grow some new habits.

YES, my friends! This is where change takes place, and new-birth begins.

In this section you will:

- ✓ Create a step by step planning system
- ✓ Record symptoms and recovery for reintegration stages
- ✓ Identify your goals and create a plan over those hurdles standing in your way
- ✓ Develop the skills to evaluate and measure growth
- ✓ Choose your steps towards relaxation and restoration

✓ Connect with your new extended family and community while continuing your journey towards the healthiest you ever!

You might think that all sounds great but just how will I do that?

You will follow a step by step guide incorporating pdf exercises guiding you each step of the way.

Identifying Your Goals and Creating a Plan

If you or someone you love is suffering from a brain injury, you know how debilitating and discouraging it can be. A life transforming and necessary step for internal recovery is the step towards self-discovery and the replacement of the limiting belief systems that cloud self-awareness and create both self-doubt and disbelief blocking recovery.

The intentions in this section are for you to discover and clarify your desires for recovery and what your personal recovery looks like.

By identifying your desires and rewriting the transcript of doubt and disbelief, replacing it with the reasons why and the road map how recovery will take place, you will have and an absolute plan towards full recovery.

I have created a powerful four part video series to help aid you with this section. Follow the YouTube links below or sign in to your membership log in and go to Chapter 15 or Bonus videos.

https://youtu.be/V5p26-FFRWA

https://youtu.be/P1-s2o5yZPc

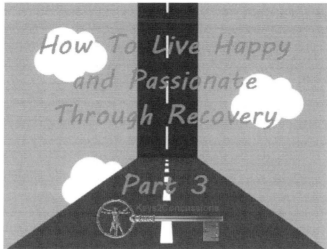

https://youtu.be/vJADUMon9UU

https://youtu.be/CTZfESqDmBc

For our **podcast listeners** you can listen to the audio on 11 major platforms. I have attached the Apple ITunes link for the Concussion podcast channel below.

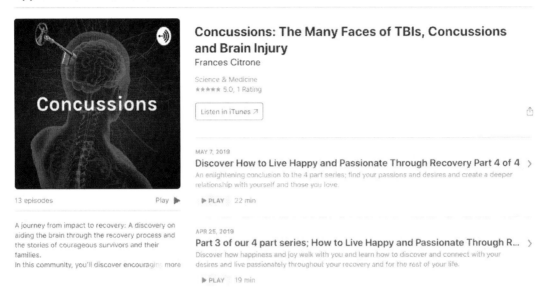

https://podcasts.apple.com/us/podcast/concussions-my-life-changing-discovery/id1440391650

Limiting Beliefs

The following exercise is intended to help define and rewrite any limiting beliefs that might be holding you back from your transformation and the most fulfilled version of you.

Follow the link to download both the instructions and exercise below, and believe that full recovery is possible. (You can access the link for extra copies or complete the exercise in print below)

Begin the recovery here: The Blog Post

Downloadable Instructions

http://www.keys2concussions.com/wp-content/uploads/2018/07/Limiting-Beliefs-Exercise-Instructions.pdf

Downloadable Exercise Worksheet

http://www.keys2concussions.com/wp-content/uploads/2017/11/Limiting-beliefs-goal-tension-diagram.pdf

Belief Systems

- Replace the belief system and rewrite the transcript of doubt and disbelief in a full recovery

- Begin the recovery here, first exercise

http://www.keys2concussions.com/the-overcome-exercise/

Limiting Beliefs Exercise Instructions

1. Consider your current situation and state underneath the blue arrow.

Writhe down your desired health, physical, and mental state in the space provided at the top up the blue arrow.

2. Moving counter clockwise, Under YOUR WHY, write why you must obtain your desired state.

3. Write the top three limited beliefs or reasons you've told yourself you cannot obtain your desired health state in the bottom left hand corner under the yellow man in chains.

4. Then re-write at least 3 replacement beliefs explaining why you can reach your desired health.

This step holds great power; re-write at least 3 replacement beliefs explaining why YOU CAN and will reach your desired health.

Feel free to print this sheet out and remind yourself of your new belief systems.

Beliefs, patterns, and behaviors are etched into your psyche and it will take a deliberate effort to retrain your mind.

Your mind is the battlefield and where the victories are won. Control and heal your mind and your thoughts and the rest will follow.

5. Create a plan of action with steps on how you can achieve your desired health.

Your action plan will incorporate your health plan, any appointments and rehabilitation steps given by your doctor, education, work, athletic and/or life integration steps all which will help you get back to your life and possibly even a more fulfilled life doing the things you love to do.

Goal and Recovery Chart

Make sure that you have listened to the <u>four part</u> video series on YouTube or Apple podcast series linked above on _Living Happy and Passionate in Recovery_ before completing this goal sheet. Without the new perspective these exercises becoming nothing more than another "to do list" you will add to your day and chances are you will not obtain that life transformation that is intended and waiting for you!

Some of you may feel like this road to recovery is an uphill battle. You may not have specific goals set, and at the moment you may not feel as optimistic as you might like to be.

For our wounded warriors and military servicemen, the journey towards recovery can bring a lot of challenges.

This next section is designed to help with that inner struggle.

This system can even be applicable for those battling severe TBI's and are left possibly learning how to walk again, talk, and perform some of the simplest tasks that many of us take for granted.

Setting specific short term and long term goals can be very beneficial in the recovery process. People who succeed at something don't merely have goals, but they have a system and a plan in reaching those goals. Create a plan with detailed steps towards each aspect of the recovery process. Also, keeping a journal recording the steps and achievements accomplished further empower the journey and add to the needed energy to persevere.

Follow this link to download your goals and recovery chart.
http://www.keys2concussions.com/goals-and-recovery-planning/

You will want multiple copies as it is an on-going journal and progressive action plan.

Date:

Daily/ Weekly/ Monthly

(Circle one)

Goal Category	Action Steps	Achievements	Lessons Learned	Self-Revelations & Epiphanies
Health & Fitness				
Career/ Education				
Personal Relationships				
Social Life				
Personal Development (Intellectual, Emotional)				
Financial (often closely connected to quality of life & other categories)				
Quality of life (Leisure, Travel, Fun & Material)				
Spiritual				
Growth & Contribution				

Keys2Eating

Symptoms and Recovery Tracker

During the healing process, it is vital to have a clear understanding as to where the patient is in their journey to recovery as well as a step-by-step plan to follow during the recovery process.

One of the best ways to define where you or the patient is in their concussion journey is through symptom tracking.

It can seem a tedious job, but it is a significant one. Follow the link below to download a symptom tracker. This will also help when determining what phase they are in for the reintegration process.

Remember for safe re-integration the patient must remain symptom-free for 24 hours before going on to the next stage and begin new activities.

This symptom record and log can also be very beneficial when you go to your follow up doctors' appointments. It is often difficult to remember the good and bad days with specifics as schedules get busy.

Select the link below to download the symptom tracker pdf.

Symptom Tracker http://www.keys2concussions.com/concussion-symptom-tracker/

You will want multiple copies to use for doctor's appointments and through recovery

Measuring Growth and Self-Evaluation

Measuring growth goes beyond just the obvious concussion symptoms. You will be able to record the reduction of concussion symptoms using the Symptom and Recover Tracker above. In this section, the focus is on measuring the inner healing of the recovery process that many people face as a result of post-concussion syndrome or PTSD.

Consider yourself or your loved one blessed if this section of the book does not apply to you.

However, that being said, for those of you that can identify with the inner challenges of your recovery process, this segment is designed for you. Do not lose hope, you are not alone nor weak, and what you are feeling is very real and quite common after a concussion or TBI.

This aspect of concussion recovery must be addressed with a well thought out plan and a proven system as all the other elements of the recovery process.

If you learn and use the techniques that I am about to teach you, you'll avoid feeling helpless and trapped in depression. This module is intended to reshape your thought patterns and help keep you moving successfully forward towards the goal of complete recovery.

While welcoming and embracing the thought pattern that life happens for us and even the challenges are gifts to help shape our destiny, you can look at your current state from a different and higher viewpoint.

By changing your view point and the angle by which you look at your situation, you can directly positively elevate your state of mind.

For instance, consider the new insights and strengths that you have already achieved since the initial concussion. Just by reading this book alone, you have increased your education on concussions, brain health, and the benefits of healthier eating.

Your new insights and strengths

- increased your education on concussions, brain health, and the benefits of healthier eating
- seen those that love you step up in support
- a new appreciation and an increased level of value placed on the magnitude of the brain and its' extensive control over the body

If you look around you, you have probably seen those that love you step up in support.

Having been through this concussion journey more than a few times with my children, coaching others through their recovery process including myself, I know I found a new appreciation and an increased level of value placed on the magnitude of the brain and its' extensive control over the body.

Take this time to slow down, be present, re-evaluate the necessities and appreciate the simple beauties of life.

Allow yourself to feel gratitude for your loved ones and the caring community around you. Receive the help and allow the relationships around you to strengthen.

Have patience with yourself. You can be so busy at being stressed out about having to rest and recover that you impede your body's ability to heal.

Prioritize your life, follow your desires/ goals road map and gift yourself health by following through with your concussion protocol meal plan.

Rest, Relaxation, and Restoration

I am sure you already know that stress is not good for you. However, you may not know just how bad and dangerous being in a constant state of stress can be.

Real physiological changes occur in the body when we are stressed.

Many of them are intended to aid the body in survival.

For example, under stress your heart begins to beat faster, your blood thickens, insulin and glucose levels are kept elevated in the body, and digestion slows down, and that is just to name a few.

Some of those might seem odd to you. Why would your body do this, and how could this be intended to aid in survival?

Picture this scenario; you happened to be living a few thousand years ago and found yourself running for your life while being chased by a lion.

Your body recognizes the stress response, so automatically begins aiding you in survival.

First, your heart beats faster to pump much-needed blood and oxygen to the muscles in your body so you can run fast and fight hard if you have to.

Second, your blood thickens and develops a clotting effect, so if you are bitten, you won't bleed to death.

Thirdly, insulin, cortisol, and glucose levels are kept elevated to provide you with the extra energy and fuel you will need to run and fight for your life.

Last but not least, you digestion stops because digestion expends a lot of energy and now is not the time for that.

There are even more physiological events that transpire during stressful situations, and many of them hurt the body when consistently induced through chronic stress.

Stress can increase inflammation in your body, make you sick by lowering your immune system, and even impede your body's ability to heal itself.

To your body, *stress is stress*.

Whether it is a lion chasing you, deadlines at work, other colleagues, that driver texting, bills and financial problems, school work, and peer pressure, or in this case, trying to recover from a concussion.

If you want to be healthy, and you want your body to be able to perform its' miraculous ability to heal itself, then you MUST relax.

Hijacking your mind and thoughts can be the most powerful tool against stress. It can also help you overcome the limiting thoughts and beliefs holding you back in any area of your life.

Meditation is a very effective way to direct your mind.

In the following exercise, I have included a relaxation meditation technique that my family personally uses within our own home.

This method has been proven to be so powerful that it is used in hypnobirthing to help manage the pain of contractions and childbirth.

Similar techniques are used to enable humans the ability to walk on glowing red fiery coals.

Relaxation Meditation

Instructions: Follow this link for a pdf version of the following meditation http://www.keys2concussions.com/relaxation-meditation-exercise/

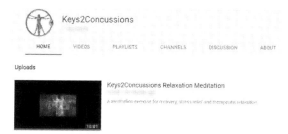

YouTube video Audio Track Link https://youtu.be/KMAVs9a7vnk

If you are the one suffering from a concussion, have someone else read the meditation below to you or listen to the audio track above.

For the following meditation, lie on your back in a dimly lit, quiet room.

{For the reader: Read with a calm, slow voice, allotting for pauses in between the words and phrases. Repeat the meditation calmly and slowly until you notice the concussed individual seems relaxed and at peace}

This meditation exercise should be done at least once a day and even multiple times if needed.

This technique can be very beneficial for and soothing for anyone during sleeplessness and restless symptoms

The Meditation:

You are feeling relaxed

5, 4, 3, 2, 1

As you take a deep breath through your nose, feel the air expand into your lungs filling your chest. Slowly exhale releasing the air through your mouth as your chest deflates. Continue those slow deep breaths inhaling through your nose and exhaling through your mouth.

Your body is beginning to feel relaxed 5-4-3-2-1

The segments of your body will now be divided into five pieces

5 - (Brief pause), your head, 4 – (brief pause), your chest, 3 – (brief pause), your abdomen, 2 – (brief pause), your hips and 1 – (brief pause), your legs through your feet

You are feeling relaxed, 5 - (pause), 4 – (pause), 3 – (pause), 2 – (pause), 1

[Continue, allowing each comma to represent a brief pause. Both the lector and receiver should be taking slow, deep, breaths.]

Feel the warmth pour over your body from your head, - 5, deep into your chest, - 4, warming your belly, - 3, through your hips, - 2, flowing down your legs, and out the bottom of your feet, – 1

You are feeling relaxed 5, 4, 3, 2, 1

Breathing, calming healing breaths

You are feeling relaxed 5, 4, 3, 2, 1

Squeeze your right hand, you are feeling relaxed 5, 4, 3, 2, 1; now release feeling the muscles relax as the blood flows through your hand

You are feeling relaxed 5, 4, 3, 2, 1

Squeeze your left hand, you are feeling relaxed 5, 4, 3, 2, 1; now release feeling the muscles relax as the blood flows through your hand

You are feeling relaxed 5, 4, 3, 2, 1

Squeeze your right arm, you are feeling relaxed 5, 4, 3, 2, 1; now release feeling the muscles relax as the blood flows through your hand

You are feeling relaxed 5, 4, 3, 2, 1

Squeeze your left arm, you are feeling relaxed 5, 4, 3, 2, 1; now release feeling the muscles relax as the blood flows through your hand

You are feeling relaxed 5, 4, 3, 2, 1

Tighten your hips, you are feeling relaxed 5, 4, 3, 2, 1; now release feeling the muscles relax as the blood flows through your hips

You are feeling relaxed 5, 4, 3, 2, 1

Tighten your legs, you are feeling relaxed 5, 4, 3, 2, 1; now release feeling the muscles relax as the blood flows through your legs

You are feeling relaxed 5, 4, 3, 2, 1

Tighten and squeeze your entire body; now release feeling the muscles relax as the blood flows through your body as you sink deeper, you are feeling relaxed 5, 4, 3, 2, 1

You are feeling relaxed 5, 4, 3, 2, 1

You are feeling relaxed 5, 4, 3, 2, 1

You are relaxed, 5, 4, 3, 2, 1

Relax, 5, 4, 3, 2, 1

Now rest

As you rest you are feeling gratitude and gratefulness for the blessings in your life

You are thankful for love

You are thankful for those who love you

You are thankful for life

You are feeling blessed

You are blessed

You are a blessing

You are feeling grateful

You are grateful

Those that love you are grateful for you

You are feeling relaxed 5, 4, 3, 2, 1

You are relaxed

Now Rest

In Closing

As you continue in your recovery journey, I want to leave you with this reflective thought.

Life happens for us, as hard as this may be to accept. Every challenge or struggle ultimately brings growth if we channel our energy in that direction.

If my son had not been a victim of three concussions, I would have never passionately written this book that you have just completed.

The beauty of life is to enjoy or find joy in the journey.

The journey with happiness being its final destination is one without life, energy, joy, and fulfillment.

Unfortunately, if you believe happiness waits for you at your destination, it will often elude you and remain in the distance like a mirage.

The closer you get to the destination, you realize happiness is not there, leaving you discouraged and looking for what other destination houses your happiness.

For some, the destination is a relationship, others a job. Many people believe that their destination for happiness is an ideal number in the bank or on the scale.

In this case, the destination might be complete brain health and full recovery.

Though the goals and vision for complete recovery are necessary to fuel the vehicle, joy and fulfillment must remain passengers on the journey with you to your destination.

Thank you for your trust and allowing the Keys2Concussions family to be a part of your journey. We would love to hear from you and share in your recovery.

 share your story.

Follow this link to **share your story and testimonials.**
http://www.keys2concussions.com/contact-us/

Thank you!

With unlimited health comes unlimited possibilities.

To learn more about total body health follow this link to our sister website Keys2Eating http://www.keys2eating.com

If you enjoy the information in this program, we would like to encourage you to show your support by sharing your testimonial with us, sharing our website with your friends and family, and supporting our continued work by considering our other programs and products.

If this book has blessed you, we would appreciate if you would take the time to
leave a review:

https://www.amazon.com/gp/product/1720126380/ref=dbs_a_def_rwt_bibl_vppi_i 3 (scroll to the bottom and select, leave a review)

May God's grace accompany you on your journey!

Disclaimer:

The techniques and advice described in this book represent the opinions of the author based on her training and experience. The author expressly disclaims any responsibility for any liability, loss or risk, personal or otherwise, which is incurred as a result of using any of the techniques, recipes or recommendations suggested herein. The responsibility for the consequences of your use of any suggestion or procedure described hereafter lies not with the authors, publisher or distributors of this book. This book is not intended as medical or health advice. If in any doubt, or if requiring medical advice, please contact the appropriate health professional. We recommend consulting with a licensed health professional before making major diet and lifestyle changes.

References

Centers for Disease Control and Prevention. (2003). *National Center for Injury Prevention and Control. Report to.* Atlanta: Centers for Disease Control and Prevention.

National Institute of Neurological Disorders and Stroke,National Institutes of Health. (2006, September 17). *Neuroprotective and disease-modifying effects of the ketogenic diet.* Retrieved from US National Library of Medicine: https://www.ncbi.nlm.nih.gov/pmc/articles/PMC2367001/

University of Illinois-Chicago, School of Medicine. (2017, March 1). *What is Ketosis?* Retrieved from Science Today: http://www.medicalnewstoday.com/articles/180858.php#the_process_of_ketosis

Alban, D. (2016, February 1). *Essential Nutrients for a Healthy Brain.* Retrieved from Brain Fit: https://bebrainfit.com/healthy-brain-nutrients/

Alzheimers Connection. (2017, January 1). *Alz Connect Ketogenic Diets.* Retrieved from Alz Connect: http://www.alz.org/search/results.asp?q=ketogenic%20diet&as_dt=i#gsc.tab=0&gsc.q=ketogenic%20diet&gsc.page=1

Andrews Institute. (2016, June 1). *The Best and Worst Foods for Concussion Recovery.* Retrieved from Andrews Institute: www.andrewsinstitute.com/news/research/articles

Brain Child Nutritionals. (2017, January 1). *Brain Child Nutritionals.* Retrieved from Brain Child Nutritionals: https://www.brainchildnutritionals.com

Brain Injury Association Staff. (2015). *Mild Brain Injury and Concussion.* Retrieved from Brain Injury Association of America: http://www.biausa.org/mild-brain-injury.htm

CDC. (2016, February 16). *Brain Injury Basics.* Retrieved from CDC: https://www.cdc.gov/headsup/basics/index.html

Children Healthcare of Atlanta. (2017, January 1). A comprehensive concussion guide. Atlanta, Georgia, USA. Retrieved from https://www.choa.org/~/media/files/Childrens/medical-services/concussion/concussion_toolkit.pdf

Cox, P. (2013). *The effects of a novel substrate on exercise energetics in elite athletes.* University of Oxford. Retrieved from http://ethos.bl.uk/OrderDetails.do?uin=uk.bl.ethos.581361

Department of Neurosurgery, David Geffen School of Medicine, University of California. (2009, april 26). *The effects of a ketogenic diet on behavioral outcome after controlled cortical impact injury in the juvenile and adult rat.* Retrieved from PubMed: https://www.ncbi.nlm.nih.gov/pubmed/19231995

Department of Neurosurgery, UCLA Brain Injury Research Center. (2009, July 26). *The effects of age and ketogenic diet on local cerebral metabolic rates of glucose after controlled cortical impact injury in rats*. Retrieved from PubMed: https://www.ncbi.nlm.nih.gov/pubmed/19226210

Departments of Neurology and Pediatrics, the Johns Hopkins Medical Institutions. (1998, December 1). *The efficacy of the ketogenic diet-1998: a prospective evaluation of intervention in 150 children*. Retrieved from PubMed: https://www.ncbi.nlm.nih.gov/pubmed/9832569

Depeartment of Health. (2016, february 1). *Shaken Baby Syndrome*. Retrieved from Depeartment of Health New York: https://www.health.ny.gov/prevention/injury_prevention/shaken_baby_syndrome/

Developing Brain. (2017, july 18). *12 Best Brain Foods to Eat Before Taking a Test*. Retrieved from Developing Brain: https://www.developinghumanbrain.org/best-brain-foods-to-eat-before-taking-a-test/

Division of Clinical Neurosciences, D. o.-2. (2016, July 15). *Human Serum Metabolites Associate With Severity and Patient Outcomes in Traumatic Brain Injury.* Retrieved from PubMed: https://www.ncbi.nlm.nih.gov/pubmed/27665050

Division of Neurology, Children's Hospital of Philadelphia. (2010, January 5). *Dietary branched chain amino acids ameliorate injury-induced cognitive impairment.* Retrieved from PubMed: https://www.ncbi.nlm.nih.gov/pubmed/19995960

Doylene. (2017, January 1). *Ketogenic Diet for Dimentia*. Retrieved from Doylene Wordpress: https://doylene.wordpress.com/2016/06/06/ketogenic-diet-for-dementia/

Faul M, X. L. (2008, January 1). *Traumatic Brain Injury in the United States: Emergency Department Visits, Hospitalizations and Deaths 2002-2006. Atlanta, GA: Centers for Disease Control and Prevention, National Center for Injury Prevention and Control.* Retrieved from CDC: https://www.cdc.gov/traumaticbraininjury/tbi_ed.html

Florey Institute of Neuroscience and Mental Health. (2012). Consensus Statement on Concussion in Sport: The 4th International Conference on Concussion in Sport, Zurich. *Consensus Statement on Concussion is Sport* (p. https://www.ncbi.nlm.nih.gov/pubmed/23479479). Zurich: NCBI.

Hamner. (2016, January 1). *Best Vitamin A*. Retrieved from Vitamins SX: http://vitaminsx.ddns.mobi/daily-vitamin-a/

Hartman. (2017, August 6). *Neuroprotection in Metabolism-Based Therapy*. Retrieved from PMC: https://www.ncbi.nlm.nih.gov/pmc/articles/PMC3245363/

Head Case Company. (2016, june 1). *Concussion InfoStats*. Retrieved from Head Case Company: http://www.headcasecompany.com/concussion_info/stats_on_concussions_sports

Heger, B. M. (2008, april 28). *Is it true I am more likely to get a concussion after already having one?* Retrieved from ScienceLine.org: http://scienceline.org/2008/04/ask-heger-concussion/

Huanshan. (2016, January 1). *Omega 3 Polyunsaturated Fatty Acids in the Brain.* Retrieved from PubMed: https://www.ncbi.nlm.nih.gov/pubmed/21622201

Jarvis, R. D. (2008). Brain Jolt: A Life Renewed After Traumatic Brain Injury, Second Edition. In R. D. Jarvis, *Brain Jolt: A Life Renewed After Traumatic Brain Injury, Second Edition.*

Jenkins, L. (2015, july 1). *Biography of Dr Johanna Budwig.* Retrieved from The Buudwig Center: http://www.budwigcenter.com/johanna-budwig-biography/#.WYDb04jyvlU

Kehr, W. (2015, 1 June). *How to Make the Budwigg Diet .* Retrieved from The Cancer Tutor: https://www.cancertutor.com/make_budwig/

Malerba, L. (2017, january 1). *Homeopathic Help for Heaed Injuries.* Retrieved from Spirit Science Healing: http://spiritsciencehealing.com/homeopathic-help-head-injuries/

Mayo Clinic. (2015, January 1). *Mayo Clinic Shaken Baby Syndrome.* Retrieved from Mayoclininc.org: http://www.mayoclinic.org/search/search-results?q=shaken%20baby%20syndrome

Mayo Clinic Staff. (2016, July 15). *http://www.mayoclinic.org.* Retrieved from Mayo Clinic: http://www.mayoclinic.org/diseases-conditions/concussion/symptoms-causes/dxc-20273155

Mayo Clinic Staff. (2016, July 15). *mayoclinic.org/diseases-conditions/post-concussion-syndrome/basics .* Retrieved from Mayo Clinic: http://www.mayoclinic.org/diseases-conditions/post-concussion-syndrome/basics

Nathan D. Zasler, M. E. (2007). Brain Injury Medicine: Principles and Practice. In M. E. Nathan D. Zasler, *Brain Injury Medicine: Principles and Practice.* Demos Medical Publishing.

NeuroSymptoms.org. (2016, July 15). *Functional and Dissociative Neurological Symptoms : a patient's guide.* Retrieved from neurosymptoms.org: http://www.neurosymptoms.org/#/post-concussion-syndrome/4582101276

Pahang. (2016, March 1). *An Observational Study of Blood Glucose Levels during Admission and 24 Hours Post-Operation in a Sample of Patients with Traumatic Injury in a Hospital in Kuala Lumpur.* Retrieved from PMC: https://www.ncbi.nlm.nih.gov/pmc/articles/PMC3328931/

Perfect Keto. (2017, January 15). *What is Ketosis.* Retrieved from Perfect Ketones: http://www.perfectketo.com/what-is-keto/

Prins, M. (2008, November 1). *DIET, KETONES AND NEUROTRAUMA.* Retrieved from PubMed: https://www.ncbi.nlm.nih.gov/pubmed/19049605

Sciences, D. o. (2013, April 15). *Human mild traumatic brain injury decreases circulating branched-chain amino acids and their metabolite levels*. Retrieved from PubMed: https://www.ncbi.nlm.nih.gov/pubmed/23560894

Silver Bulletin. (2017, January 1). *Silver Bulletin Utopia Silver*. Retrieved from SilverBulletin: http://silverbulletin.utopiasilver.com/

Sports Concussion Institute. (2017, January 1). *Concussions*. Retrieved from Sports Concussion Institute: http://concussiontreatment.com/resources/

Swanson, A. (2017, January 1). *The Best Supplements for Concussion Recovery*. Retrieved from Paleo Edge: http://paleoedge.com/how-nutrition-can-help-concussions/

The Truth About Cancer. (2017, January 1). *How the Budwig Diet Protocol Works*. Retrieved from The Truth About Cancer: https://thetruthaboutcancer.com/budwig-diet-protocol-cancer/

WebMd. (2016, January 1). *What is Ketosis?* Retrieved from WebMD: http://www.webmd.com/diabetes/type-1-diabetes-guide/what-is-ketosis#1

Mayo Clinic Staff. (2016, July 15). *http://www.mayoclinic.org*. Retrieved from Mayo Clinic: http://www.mayoclinic.org/diseases-conditions/concussion/symptoms-causes/dxc-20273155